CHANGING THE GAME

ANGE POSTECOGLOU

with Andy Harper

CHANGING THE GAME

Football in Australia through my eyes

MICHAEL JOSEPH
an imprint of
PENGUIN BOOKS

MICHAEL JOSEPH

UK | USA | Canada | Ireland | Australia
India | New Zealand | South Africa | China

Penguin Books is part of the Penguin Random House group of companies
whose addresses can be found at global.penguinrandomhouse.com.

Penguin
Random House
Australia

First published by Penguin Random House Australia Pty Ltd, 2016

1 3 5 7 9 10 8 6 4 2

Text copyright © Ange Postecoglou 2016

The moral right of the author has been asserted.

Cover design by Adam Laszczuk © Penguin Random House Australia Pty Ltd
Text design by Samantha Jayaweera © Penguin Random House Australia Pty Ltd
Front cover photographs: players by Asanka Brendon Ratnayake/Anadolu Agency/Getty
Images; Ange Postecoglou by Brendon Thorne/Getty Images
Back cover photograph by Brendon Thorne/Getty Images
All photographs in the picture section courtesy of Ange Postecoglou, unless otherwise credited
Typeset in Sabon by Samantha Jayaweera, Penguin Random House Australia Pty Ltd
Colour separation by Splitting Image Colour Studio, Clayton, Victoria
Printed and bound in Australia by Griffin Press, an accredited ISO AS/NZS
14001 Environmental Management Systems printer.

National Library of Australia
Cataloguing-in-Publication data:

Postecoglou, Ange, author
Changing the game / Ange Postecoglou, Andy Harper
9780143797159 (paperback)

Postecoglou, Ange
Soccer – Australia
Soccer players – Australia – Biography

Other Creators/Contributors:
Harper, Andy, author

796.33466092

penguin.com.au

CONTENTS

CONTENTS

Preface

When the idea of writing a book was suggested to me, my first thought was that there was still a fair bit to be told. In other words, I felt there was still meaningful stuff ahead of me that I hadn't experienced yet. The discussion then went to whether the timing was right for me to give my thoughts on the state of the game and, more roundly, how the game has shaped my leadership model and my management style. That was of interest to me, as I am constantly being asked to deliver talks on these topics and, inevitably, they are intertwined with my love of the game.

A part of me wanted to write this book entirely by myself, as I have always found jotting down my thoughts and observations to be very therapeutic. The reality was that time, my biggest enemy in any venture, was never going to allow me the opportunity for that therapy. I needed to entrust this most vital part of the process to another writer.

Andy Harper, or Harps as I know him, was for me

the only person capable of writing my words. Harps, a Sydney-born, bush-loving Aussie, and me, a Greek-born immigrant whose only experience of Aussie life came in suburbia. Who would have thought that we would be kindred spirits in many respects? But that is the beauty of the game.

When things seemed fairly bleak after my tenure as coach of the Young Socceroos, Harps was one person who took time out to make sure I was not lost to the game. While I'm eternally grateful for that faith, it's his passion and insight for the game that has fuelled our subsequent friendship. I owe him and his beautiful family thanks for sharing their country home with me so that the two of us could write what, we thought, was going to be a book about nothing. Hopefully it is a lot more than that.

The game in Australia has had challenges, but I firmly believe that its ability to unite and inspire will lead this country to a new level of self-worth and identity. Wait till we win a World Cup!

1
BOY IN A BUBBLE

Football isn't something I came to later in life. I wasn't a kid who dabbled in lots of stuff throughout school and adolescence, looking for meaning. From as early as I can remember, football has provided me with the answers I need. Football was the thing through which I made sense of life, where I created my world and my identity. I was gripped by the game's beauty. I was in awe of the game's masters and would swoon in their presence, just like all the other kids. But as I reflect, and as I now understand myself, I see that my love of football has always gone deeper than that. Football brought me closer to my father, and that was the relationship I craved. Through football and my father, in the swirling circumstances of migrant life, my life's patterns emerged.

I was born in Athens, Greece, in 1965. My dad had a pretty successful business. He came from a line of merchants and furniture makers. He used to make children's furniture, toys, cradles and that sort of thing. As far as I'm aware, it was a pretty pain-free and middle-of-the-road existence. But around 1969, as the government commenced its acquisition, or nationalisation, of land and businesses – including my parents' – the agitation to look somewhere else began. In a very short space of time, my family went from being settled to being very exposed. My father's ability to provide for his family was evaporating.

It's amazing how people react to such acute circumstances. My uncle tells a story from an earlier time when my dad won a lottery. It wasn't a big prize but, in comparative terms, it was a significant amount. It was in my dad's nature to share the winnings around. But when the government went into repossession mode, and he was in need, none of those people were forthcoming with help. Maybe they had their own issues, I can't say. But my dad felt abandoned by those around him, by the community he'd been a part of and in which he'd felt secure. My parents were like a shag on the rock.

At one point he and my uncle upped and went to Libya to work in construction. He would go anywhere to work. Apparently there were times when he wouldn't be sure if he even had safe passage back to Greece, back to us. But he'd worry about that later. For the meantime, the money was far better than he'd get in Greece, and the family's welfare had to be secured. We were part of a remittance economy. Parents working abroad and sending earnings back home to their families. I see a lot of that sort of thing now as I travel through Asia with the Socceroos and can't help but feel empathy. As I fly into and drive by these communities, and am served in hotels by expat remittance workers, I wonder how their kids are being shaped, as I was, by that separation and transience.

My dad was an independent thinker. He would refuse the idea that he had to accept the circumstances that had befallen him simply because they had befallen him, and that was part of his drive to go work abroad. His hand may have been forced by the government, but he was willing to go anywhere to see what possibilities existed.

Emigration was one of those possibilities. When I was five years old and my sister, Elizabeth, was ten, my family was presented with two options: South Africa and Australia. My dad chose Australia, with really no idea what it was or where it was. Unlike many, we didn't have family already here. We didn't have friends here. We had no pre-existing network of anything here. He just made the decision to come to Australia. The fact that there were a lot of Greeks here, particularly in Melbourne, would have filtered through to him even in those pre-internet times, but apart from that it may as well have been Mars, for all he knew.

From the moment we arrived, he got into cabinet making and carpentry, the skills of his trade, and began piecing together a new life. Importantly he also plunged straight into the local Greek community, the largest of its kind outside of Greece itself. Really, there was no other option. None of my family spoke English. It wasn't as though we got off the boat and were funnelled into any help centres or Australia 101 classes. Folk like us landed laid bare, exposed to the elements. You made do.

We were sponsored by another Greek family. We didn't know them. It wasn't a particularly warm connection but neither was it traumatic. In our new life in Australia, that family and the Greeks of Prahran were the extent of our world. You have to be in such a situation, with no language access to the community, to really understand how debilitating it is, how dehumanising. It wasn't just a man, his wife and his kids in a restaurant where they couldn't read the menu; it was a vulnerable family, arriving in a new country to start a new life. There was no way in. No familiarity. You could only really go as far as language could take you, and that was in and around the local Greek community.

My sister started school as soon as we got to Australia. It must have been tremendously difficult and would have been a very formative experience. She was at a vulnerable age and in an environment that was too often hostile to new arrivals, and particularly those who didn't speak English. I was put into child-minding because Mum had to get working too. She did every-thing, although mainly she worked as a machinist. We bought a sewing machine and she was always mending or making clothes.

My dad remembers the first bed they acquired. It was soon after we arrived. He'd heard that somebody was giving away a mattress, a double-bed mattress. So he and the dad from the other family we lived with trudged off one Saturday morning to get the new bed. It was going for free so it was a must. They had an address for the pick-up but that's all. No car and no map, or at least not any Greek-language road maps. As they wove through the streets, somehow, they found the house with the bed. After clean-and-jerking the thing above their heads, they soon realised they couldn't remember how to get home. They were so focused on finding the place, they'd forgotten the route they'd taken. These two men were left walking the streets, hot, frustrated and lost, with no means of asking for directions or help, unable to take public transport, and certainly no smart phone with GPS to take them back from whence they'd come. They'd pass the same landmarks and realise they were walking in circles. It was getting dark, they were getting tired, but finally they made it home. My dad collapsed on his new bed in the entrance hall. It's a story that's stayed with me because it's a bit of a metaphor, really, of their existence at the time.

Without the support of the Greek community one wonders how we would have survived. There was no arrival kit telling us, 'Well, this is how you assimilate to life here.' It's pretty humiliating. Probably the Aussies looking on, with no appreciation of what and who these people were, would sit and judge two migrant blokes wandering through the suburbs of Melbourne with a pre-loved bed on their shoulders. Who are these blokes? Vagrants? There's no knowledge of their past or their achievements or their skill. They're just hopelessly lost, struggling like drunken sailors after a session on the rum to keep aloft a free bed.

It's not a unique story but, as I look back, it's just so far removed from the sort of life my own kids have, and even how my sister and I lived as teenagers. The early part of my life makes me shake my head; it's surreal, just totally different. It wasn't until we moved out of the two-bedroom house we shared with that other family and into our own place that we started making our own family friends, settled into some sort of routine Australian life – whatever that is or was – and started living in a way that bears any resemblance to now.

Naturally, however, having made the difficult transition to a more normal and familiar existence didn't mean that the struggles were over. Even after securing more stability, I can remember my parents sitting with their heads in their hands questioning the wisdom of their decision to leave Greece.

Mum was a bit more resilient but I know my dad struggled a lot, which is interesting because he had been the prime mover for us leaving Greece in the first place. The circumstances there made him feel that he had to look for a better life for his family. But what is a better life? What does that mean? I can ask that now, almost philosophically, although I'm sure my parents wrestled with those questions as they wrestled with the difficulties of migration. As bad as things were in Greece, Dad still had a network of friends and he still had the ability to socialise. Even surrounded by instability and with diminishing material means, he at least had familiar reference points, people and culture to sustain him. In Melbourne he could work and provide, but everything else seemed like a mad scramble, like he was walking on ball bearings. The social network here was limited. The nature of my parents' work meant that they were largely estranged from the broader Greek community so, as replenishing as it was when they had that contact, it wasn't every day. The work was constant but they were quite alone and isolated. If they needed a solution for something they had to find it themselves, without the assistance of the internet. There was plenty of frustration and many times the conversation turned to going back to Greece. I think it was in Dad's mind that ultimately that was what would happen. That was his hankering. For him the ideal life was in Greece, back when things were going well, and if he could just get over this hump in Australia and get ahead, he could go back to the comforts of Greece. Australia, for him, was missing that very important component, not just survival but enjoying life. It gnawed at him constantly.

As time went on it became clear how focused Mum had to be to keep our life in Australia going. Aware of the sacrifices and upheaval we'd experienced, retuning to Greece just didn't make sense to her. It was such an uncertain place economically and politically. She didn't become less Greek because she came to Australia, but she most certainly felt that for her kids this was a much better place than the one they'd left.

Home wasn't always a happy environment. My sister was starting to get into her teens at the same time as she was getting into the Australian way of life. The old European mentality of how a daughter should behave and with whom she should spend her time became battlegrounds. My dad's perennial state of tiredness was an additional irritant. I'd wake up in the morning and he'd already have left for work, and at night he'd come home, have dinner, and crash into that pre-owned bed. Intermittently he'd raise an eye, and sometimes his voice, to challenge my sister. It was very wearing for all of us.

My mum was constantly counting the pennies to make sure everything was paid and up to date. Part of me was oblivious to what was going on but, equally, my recollection is clear enough to know that unease was our constant bedfellow. It was always pretty tense. But I'd be outside playing, or insulating myself in some other way from the lack of peace.

By the time I was seven or eight, and we'd been in the country for a couple of years, I remember football starting to take centrestage in my life. Football was really the only thing that relaxed my father, and time in its company was precious for him. Maybe it was because at the football he was surrounded by people who had the same sort of issues, the same dilemmas, all of them just there to enjoy the game and get a weekly release from the ordeal of being a stranger in a strange land. Eating and speaking Greek, the shared experiences of migration, a common language to give expression to those frustrations – one can imagine how powerful an analgesic that was. Being able to find a public toilet, or at least asking for directions to one in your mother tongue was, in fact, an enlivening experience.

The football provided a two-hour block every Sunday where all those daily impediments were gone. The things that should be simple in life, but were complicated in Australia, fell into place at the football. To me, even getting into the car and driving to the ground, my father seemed different. It was only a few hours a week, but before and after a game the atmosphere at home would change. The anticipation he was feeling lifted the pall from all of us. It was like we could breathe. You can imagine how important that became.

My dad loved the game of football as well as the experience of the football. He loved talking about it. Invariably, after games we'd go back to someone's house and the dads would all sit around the table, dissecting the game, abusing the coach, ripping into the referee, celebrating players and goals and moves. All my mates would be outside playing but I'd sit at the table with the 'old' men, sitting next to my old man,

Most of that stuff was beyond a kid and certainly beyond us. But with football I could have a discussion with him, he would talk about it with me almost as an equal. We'd speculate on the team on the way to the ground, the strength of the opposition, who'd win and by how much. And then after the game why we'd won or lost, who'd contributed and who hadn't. I kept on it and I kept with it and I kept digging and prompting and responding; I sensed the connection was real and I wanted more. At that point football was a means to an end, but my desire for my father's attention and company was the precursor to my own love for the game.

At the post-match get-togethers, I'd sit next to Dad and sometimes he'd say, 'Piss off and go and play with the other kids,' but I wasn't going anywhere. I was where I wanted to be, where I needed to be: with him. Sometimes I wonder if the 'piss off' line was a decoy. To be seen to do what the other dads and sons were doing. I wonder if he didn't actually prefer me being there with him. I wonder if he knew, or sensed, that I wasn't going to leave, but would say it anyway, safe in the knowledge that the bond wouldn't break. And in refusing the request, I was in some way pushing a boundary, testing the resistance.

My sister says I pay him too much credit. But part of his master plan was the reality of this foreign country, what it meant and how it could be used. He didn't and listen. I loved listening to them. I learned a lot. My father got right into it. I would rarely see him so animated as at these times. Perhaps only when he was at loggerheads with my sister. I was realising that football was something much more to him than just a way to pass the time.

The teams of the Melbourne Greek community, like our South Melbourne Hellas, were more than just football clubs. We'd go to church on Sunday morning and then again in the afternoon at South. Holy church and football church was where people like my father got the peace and meaning and sustenance that were so elusive for them during their working week.

There can be little doubt that part of my initial attachment to football was because of the connection it gave me with Dad. Starved of contact with him during the week, I could, at the football, get into what he was into. I could bind myself to him, become an extension of him. I'm convinced that was the initial source of my engagement with the game. It wasn't about football per se, because I wanted to fit into the bigger 'Australian' scheme of things too. I played cricket and Aussie Rules at school. But I wanted to connect with Dad, and football was the thing, the vessel on board which there was room for both of us. I couldn't discuss his work with him, or Greece, and god knows the family goings-on were in no way the business of a young son.

uproot his family and come to Australia on a whim. He found it very difficult at times to see through the haze that was his confusing life. He didn't know anything about Australia, and learning and adapting was a slow process. But despite the pull of his homeland, there was a reason for coming to the other side of the world. His kids were crucial to him. Through us he could satiate the paternal desire to nurture, but through us he could also build some cultural scaffolding that made him feel comfortable. And then for us, his family, the reasons for coming would materialise. But he really struggled with my sister. He'd wrack his brains about how to keep her close to him, close to his values and culture. But with me the answer was obvious. He loved seeing that I was beginning to love football, and it was something he understood, so he became determined that I be surrounded by it.

Every one of his friends was Greek and all their kids were going to do Greek things. The family background of each of them was, for all intents and purposes, the same. The life journey was the same, the values were the same, and if he could organise the surroundings properly, his son wouldn't have the desire, or need, to go beyond those boundaries. It was his way of delivering me safely to the times when I'd be responsible for myself. The local school we attended was out of his reach – who are these Australian kids? He could exert no control over that. I wasn't allowed to hang out with the Brads and Shanes of Prahran. He didn't know them and had no sense of what made them as people. Were they honest, respectful? Did their parents let them roam the streets? What did they eat? All that stuff. But with Nick and Manny and Chris and Kosta he was okay, because he knew them without having to meet them. My dad was no dill, far from it. But he, like so many other migrants, was in survival mode. He was grabbing onto whatever he could reach and hanging on for dear life. Greek culture was that life raft.

Anyway, forty years after all my father's attempts at social engineering, I'm still best mates with those kids. The people he pushed me toward are still my friends today. He threw me in with them and I haven't deviated. I look at all their lives and they're all successful, solid citizens. I sit back and wonder if this was all part of his grand plan. Was it luck or good management? The sentiments of my sister echo again; maybe I do give him too much credit. My dad focused on what he could control, and even struggled against what he couldn't. In me, he sensed he could feed this passion for football and simultaneously mould me into the person he wanted, to guard against outside influence and mini-mise risk.

Going to Greek school on a Saturday was another part of the equation. A lot of kids did it. A lot of kids from other cultures had their Saturday school too. The Greek-Australian experience wasn't unique and the formula for assimilation was shared across the migrant spectrum. There was no question about the family commitment to Greek school, but inevitably at some point it would clash with football. When I was ten or eleven, I was selected into a regional football team. I'm a bit hazy on the details of the team and the competition, but for me the real thing was that football collided head-on with Saturday Greek school. In normal circumstances – mine and other families' – education would come first. But my old man, without a hint of hesitation, said no to Greek school and yes to the football. This, for me, was a seminal moment. He understood the football world and what that world could do for me and, importantly, what it was doing for the two of us.

In many ways my dad was taking the road less travelled. Certainly more people remain in the place of their birth than emigrate. And probably most migrant Greek families would have made their kids eschew rep football teams for Saturday Greek school. Statistics would also say that most Greek kids' families slipped into 'Aussie' sports as opposed to remaining with the Greek community clubs. The influence of the Greek community on Australian football, and certainly in Melbourne, remains distinctive and strong. But while there are almost half a million Greeks in Melbourne, the numbers make it clear that the majority of them aren't circulating around their original cultural hubs, the football clubs. Those circumstances made my dad an outlier for prioritising football, at least in part.

Going down such a road isn't a completely cavalier exercise though. It certainly wasn't for us. Even if the course and the destination weren't clear, decisions were still being made according to things that are important and sustaining. As I consider my father's choices, it was about understanding that this uncertain road, Australia, could be traversed only in a sturdy vehicle with a working gear box, Greek culture. It wasn't just for the sake of doing something different, and hanging it all out there was nonsense too; there was, and had to be, a reason behind it and structure around it.

For my dad the reason was to provide a better material life for his family. But the means by which he would do that was shaping his son through football, and the networks it provided. Football allowed him to construct a family that maintained some familiarity but also set down some markers in this new country. If we were in Greece football would still have been in the family but it mightn't have had the significance of our experiences here. Because when I look back it wasn't just the aesthetics and fandom, it was that process of consolidation and immersion that bound me so deeply to football. In turn, that attachment accelerated my fascination with the game's mechanics. In that sense it was a virtuous cycle.

In many ways, for me to go down to the oval to play footy and cricket with the local kids would have been easier for all of us. Many migrant kids took that path. For me, too, opportunities and friendships would have come from that. But my dad held close to him the values and ideals that were dear to him, and footy and cricket didn't fit in. In his mind it was important not to change direction or yield. At the time I didn't appreciate why I wasn't encouraged to play local games on the local oval with the local kids, but I do now.

This is the important role, then, that clubs like South Melbourne Hellas played for young kids in the community. Without the encouragement to play local games – or in some instances without the permission to do so – young migrants had to be provided with something else to which they could cleave. This was the beauty of those clubs like Hellas and Heidelberg. They weren't just football clubs and they were special because of that. When, in the latter years of the National Soccer League (NSL), they had become just another sporting club, they also lost their essence. Because they wanted to fit in with the larger society they forgot why they were around in the first place, the things that made them unique. There were reasons why a person would get off a boat in a foreign country and go to the football ground before anywhere else. When these clubs still had strong identities, as they did during my upbringing, they played an enduring role for families like mine. They helped parents make it through. There are probably many reasons for it, but over time clubs like South seemed to lose the idea of why there were doing what they were doing. Perhaps people grew out of the need for them, too. The newer generations were assimilated. But at that time, for my dad, South held the same clear idea of purpose as him, and the strength that came from that was vital.

It's true that Australia is an easier place now. Things were less nuanced then. We weren't living in a global world, as such. My parents didn't know what Australia was like before they came. Making the same journey now is softened by the comparative smallness of today's world. But for my family there was nothing. Emigration was a massive leap of faith and desperation, and as far as any of them knew there was no safety net at the other end. The unknown was, for my dad, a real battle, so his fallback position was to keep close some of the old ways. Never let the safety of familiarity be too far away. Every decision had to measure against that. The paradox was that the attendant comforts of Greekness were matched by the angst of attempting to fit in; he couldn't let go of the things from which he was trying to get away and he couldn't, or wouldn't, grab onto the handles of the new society.

My personality adapted to this reality. I was a compliant kid. I would have struggled if I wasn't. I didn't want to be in the constant struggle my sister was, both because it looked unpleasant and because I wanted my father's company. My sister was a lot more headstrong than me, something that was perhaps exacerbated by her being thrown into school as soon as we arrived. That must have been a sink or swim experience. And, in learning to swim, she railed against dad's values. She'd take him on. She just wanted to do what the other kids were doing. She wanted to have male friends; the other kids did, so she was going to as well. He would have seen it as an act of defiance but to her it would have been a way of staying afloat in her world. So I played the role, I thought, of balance in the family. Doing everything right, being good, not causing a fuss or at least not adding to the tension. I tried to do well at school, never got into trouble or provided problems or headaches.

I focused on my football. I wanted the approval of the household. I constantly tried to make Mum and Dad happy with everything I was doing. Observing the grating between my sister and my father, I knew that if I was the same that might have tipped him over the edge. He might have thrown in the towel, admitting defeat, packing up the bags and taking us back to Greece. But in me he must have seen a ray of light, the reason why he and Mum had chosen to come here. That it could work, both worlds side by side.

At the time I didn't understand why I was that way, because outside the family I struggled with authority. Not so that it showed – I kept quiet about it, internalised it, processed it. But I had issues with teachers and coaches or anyone who'd tell me what to do. I look at my dad and sister and think it must be something in our DNA. Every time someone told me what to do it almost irrevocably broke down that relationship. I couldn't handle others assuming such a position, yet in the household that is all I was doing, vigilantly peacekeeping.

I was aware of the stresses of migrant life, but was also settling in and enjoying Australia. As time moved on, I found myself wanting less and less to do with Greek things and rebelled accordingly, apart from the football of course. I had a terrible surname, a real impediment to life in the 1970s and '80s. People couldn't say my name and some would relish that. I hated Greek music, speaking Greek, everything about all of it. The thought of us heading back there sent shivers through me. But return we did, in 1975, because Dad's mum passed away. I couldn't wait to get out of the place. I couldn't understand the people there, what they were about. The language was now hard for me.

The prospect of leaving Australia was something I couldn't countenance. So I took it upon myself to show the family this was where we needed to be. It was good for me and it was good for everyone else. Bizarrely, that rift between me and Greece stayed with me until my early to mid-twenties. I didn't want to know at all back then, didn't want to go there even for a holiday. Yet later in life Greece probably draws me in more than anything else.

I look back on this internal struggle and realise that it was perhaps my first experience of trying to influence an environment. Was it early leadership? When I was eight or nine years old, there was definitely a need to control and influence. An understanding that, even at a young age, that was possible. And for me once that registered, that me doing and saying certain things controlled certain outcomes, that I could affect those around me in this way, it became a key driver. Subconscious maybe, certainly at first, but I reckon that's why I had a problem with authority outside the home. Rather than act the rebel, or indulge in any outbursts, I internalised my dissension, which at times took quite a bit of effort. People telling me what to do, rather than me being the one to guide or influence or have a say in something – I just couldn't relate. It wasn't as though I was 'having a say' on the home front, but the relationships within our family were the levers and keeping the peace was me exerting control over them. Making sure that nothing drastic, like going back to Greece, would take place.

This battle was very much internal. I was still very conscious that I had to be a good boy. Maybe internalising so much so young is what has allowed me, as an adult, to close up shop and keep my distance from people. I'm notorious for that. When I was younger I learned to keep my own counsel, make my own assessments, bite my tongue, let situations ride and watch interactions take their course. I wasn't keeping the peace for the sake of it but for a specific outcome I had in mind. It was relationship poker. And I learned pretty quickly that people can't help but blink first.

Of course any sort of action against authority outside the household would get back to my father and I was paranoid about that. As a ten-year-old, figuring out how I was going to get control of a situation without arousing anger or suspicion is a pretty complex thing. How does a kid chart a course through that?

Football was my answer. Once I'd figured that out I was away. As a child I felt I understood the game and, I think, to a higher level than anyone else I knew. I'd been sitting around men talking about the game for years. The pieces were being put in place. From my position of greater knowledge I could start to take control. So in Year 7, at Prahran High School, as a twelve-year-old, I became the coach of our team. There hadn't been a soccer team before and we, the migrant kids, put a team together. But with no precedent at the school there was nothing in place to get us going. That was my chance. The music teacher was the coach and he'd be marking homework when we were supposed to practise. So I took over as coach. My first gig. For our playing kit we got the hand-me-downs from the school footy team from the year before. But at least we had a team and I was coach. The team photo says 'Player/ Coach, Ange Postecoglou'.

It was a bit strange really, in hindsight, having a twelve-year-old kid running the show. Stranger again that the kids would even listen to me. But it didn't seem strange then. It seemed very natural. My mates in that team are still my mates today. They ask me now, 'Why the hell were we listening to you back then? We don't understand.'

We were all the same age. I had no experience as a coach, only those years of sitting around the older guys listening to them talk. But the team, my peers, listened. I must have made sense. I'd tell them who'd play what position, who'd take free kicks and what system we'd play, the whole box and dice. And they listened. I planned training sessions, explained exercises, organised tactics. And they kept listening.

Once I'd tapped into this new world, I didn't look back. It didn't worry me any more that I didn't have control over teachers because I was running this team. That little world, all of a sudden, was mine. I knew that whether it was an older kid or an adult I was talking to, in that scenario I was in control. It became like a drug. I loved it. I'd get twenty cents lunch money and I'd use eight cents of it buying the *Herald Sun* so I could read about the game, although there wasn't much coverage at the time. I'd read the back pages, the other sports, gleaning any relevant information, but football was the thing. Can you imagine a young kid walking around with the newspaper folded up under his arm? You'd look at it today and think there was something wrong. But in the morning the first thing I needed to do was read about what was going on, beyond just seeing the scores and results. It became an obsession. It wasn't just playing, it was different. Players just love to play but that wasn't enough for me. I created a whole new world, a make-believe football world, but one that was absolutely real to me.

From the school's point of view I was filling a coaching void created by these migrant kids' decision to form a team. They had no means, or desire really, to fill that void, so I was a convenient option. But it wasn't so straightforward to me. The coaching wouldn't have lasted otherwise. I wasn't any more mature than any of the other kids and couldn't have stayed focused on the job if I was just filling in for the music teacher. The school decided pretty quickly just to let things keep on. I must have been convincing. A twelve-year-old speaking with the conviction and wisdom of a forty- or fifty-year-old man, because they were my instructors. Importantly, I wasn't simply regurgitating things I'd heard others say. That would have had a very short life expectancy too. I was surrounded by a cohort of kids who loved the game as much as I did. The difference between them and me was that the intricacies and layers of the game and coaching were already a fascination of mine, over and above just playing, which was the other kids' focus. I was pretty introverted socially but in the coaching context I came into my own. Coaching that team was never in doubt for me.

One of the guys, still a close mate of mine today, tells of the time in that first year when we had to vote for the captain of the team. Everyone just assumed it was going to be me but he insisted on a vote. Greeks and democracy and all that. He said, 'No, no, why is it that you're always going to be captain? We're going to have a vote.' So the team had a vote and it ended up being unanimous in my favour. I asked my mate what that was all about.

'Yeah, I voted for you as well. I just wanted to see.' He still doesn't understand why he voted for me or the unanimous result, but says, 'You had a way of convincing us that you should be in charge.' And I felt comfortable. In another social context I would have slid into the background but in football front and centre was the only place for me to be.

It wasn't as though I was embarking on a career then. There was no feeling, in those times and in this country, that one could make a career out of football. It was different for youngsters coming through Aussie Rules, the best kids in that sport were scouted early and the path was set for them at schools and clubs. The talent would have been groomed and nurtured. Football didn't offer that, so it wasn't about making an early career decision. It was the feeling of controlling an environment and enjoying the thrill of people responding to it that was stimulating me. And not just control for its own sake, either, but control to create a better end point.

———

The National Soccer League started in 1977 and there was a sense of how special it was, but it was still only semi-professional. The newspaper coverage was still buried a few pages in from the back, in the sport section but nestled next to the funeral notices. (Unfortunately sometimes it was the clubs who were the subject of a funeral notice.) It was understood that Aussie Rules and cricket dominated.

I remember in Grade 5 winning the award for most improved in the school Aussie Rules team. I brought it home and put it on the dinner table so Dad could see it when he arrived home from work. He walked in and sat down; weary, hungry and spent, just wanting to eat. He saw the trophy, a statuette of a guy taking a mark. The shape of the ball was unmistakable.

'What's this?' he asked. I told him, and a moment of silence followed.

He pushed himself out from the table and told me to get the ball, we were going outside for a kick. Dinner was suspended. For the next half-hour I received a tutorial on passing a round ball with my weaker left foot. For me that was both deflating and inspiring. The message, however, was clear.

He didn't want to lose me to activities for which he had no affinity. He couldn't guide my course if that happened, and to him that would have been unacceptable. I understood that football was very much a niche and I held onto it even more for that reason. I might have been marked as a kid with Aussie Rules potential, but that wasn't for me because at the time it wasn't for Dad either. I understood that intuitively. Earning credit in the eyes of my dad was key to everything. As peripheral as football was in Australia, I was going to make it somehow, in my world and on my terms.

Coaching became a constant from there on. I understood the game and was also learning how to work the personalities. Others couldn't see the attraction of that. Kids were supposed to enjoy running around and playing. I did that too, but I always needed something more. Others would wonder why a kid would want to ostracise himself and be a coach. But I got a buzz from it. My mates were happy to let me go because it meant they didn't have to worry about it. I was happy to think about training and put out the cones and set the field, they didn't want to do any of that. To them that was a burden but for me it was like walking into the light. I was creating the world and I would be giving the orders. Even as a young player I couldn't just do what I was told on the field, I needed to know why I was being asked to do something. My Under 9s coach at South Melbourne, the first year I joined the club, was a 'just do it' coach. That was never enough for me so I'd pester him after training and games. When the other kids were getting stuck into the oranges, I'd be trying to pick his brains about how the game went. I think my mates in the team were willing to accept that was just who I was.

There was not a minute in the day where I didn't think about football. I remember buying every magazine that had something football about it. *Roy of the Rovers*, *Shoot*, *Match*. They'd be three months old, imported from the UK, and I'd run to the newsagents to get them as they hit the stands. Mum would send me to the milk bar to get something and I'd take a tennis ball and kick and dribble it all the way there and back. At home I'd create my own games. I'd try to entice my sister to play but she wouldn't indulge me. It was a full-blown obsession and I literally created a world of my own. I was, I guess, like a boy in a bubble. It was the one part of my life where I was master and in control. It was also, I guess, a port in the storm that was raging all around me.

That sort of visualisation is important. When going down the road less travelled you've got to get into the habit of imagining a path or an outcome, or series of outcomes, that can accumulate over time. What's something going to look like? For me, these pictures have always been very vivid. I had a clear idea of what the picture was, even if for others in Australia back then the concepts were foreign. The world I was envisaging – of robust professional football with all the debates and pressures and tensions and joys – didn't exist here, not yet anyway, but that didn't stop me creating it in my mind. People would say, 'How are you going to do that here? What you're talking about doesn't exist,' and that resistance fired me up and would fuel even greater, clearer imagination. These were stories that I was constantly developing; I was substituting myself for the big names of world football as they'd win trophies. I could see it happening. My mind was awash with them. They were very real to me.

I think that sort of dreaming, and commitment to a dreaming, is necessary. Of course it's a lot easier when you know what the end point is going to be; 'I'm going to play Aussie Rules footy,' for example. That's all here in Australia, contained and tangible. Maybe that doesn't require as vivid a dreaming. It's not so much the road less travelled as a six-lane highway that's fully signposted. But the more obscure the end point, as was the case with me, the more important the dreaming. For me to have said I want to coach at a World Cup, how was that going to happen? But that's the sort of picture I played out in my mind endlessly, over many years. A young Australian migrant kid of Greek background, thinking grandiose things like that, is surely certifiable. Or so the thinking went. Sometimes, though, unless you're prepared to step away from the accepted path, the remarkable outcome will remain elusive and life will remain mundane. I look back and see how my parents stepped away from the accepted path, many times, and good things came as a result. I have no doubt that observing and experiencing that has programmed me to take the same approach. I've found the results invigorating.

It's probable, in my mind, that everyone has the chance to obsess about something in a meaningful and constructive way. It's about being open and honest with yourself so that you're able to realise when you're approaching the decision point between playing it safe or following that obsession into the unknown. I believe that's where real discovery and life is. There wasn't anything unique in my upbringing. Even the difficult parts, well, plenty of people can regale with variations on the same themes. And the thing that lights the fire inside – if it's not universally accepted or there's no clearly defined path to pursuing it, there will be a lot of forces deflecting you off course. Or making you bypass it completely. There'll be the inevitable questions about the potential for a career or income, and if there isn't, then why bother? Or, where does that end up? These junctures in life are not always embraced. Many people get intimidated by them. Too often the opportunity for growth and achievement is lost and people miss the chance to do what, for them, would have been something special. Conservatism kicks in, the safe option is taken. But the numbers don't add up. A lack of confidence subsumes the thought processes. Convention is easier, and certainly less confronting, but the search for acceptance dulls the senses to possibility.

You know when you're on that special journey because you don't really care where it's going to end up. Simply being *on* that journey is everything. You're not doing something necessarily because of the end point but because it feeds you. There is no concern about acceptance, approval, vindication or some sort of kicker at the end of it all. When you get into that space you should know that when everything else might be telling you not to continue, that's when you hang on. That it's exactly what you're meant to be doing.

Obsession doesn't equate to easy street, though. The reality is that, when you invest as much as is needed to give life to these dreams, heartbreak is almost inevitable. This game, football, I know is going to break my heart. If you're distracted at all, you'll walk away. But if you've never known anything else and the dreams of this journey have been feeding you since day dot, you're never going to walk away.

I've not walked away at any stage. When the game

did break my heart I didn't think about doing something else because I didn't know and couldn't conceive of anything else. The pictures that have been created in my head since I was ten years old weren't going to be erased by disappointing circumstances. So I remained, and have found my way through.

That's a bit like my dad. He didn't have a choice other than working to keep me close to his culture. That was his dreaming. That was how he planned for us to survive migration. He didn't know anything else. It was physically tiring, culturally exacting and emotionally draining. But he stayed with what he knew and the course plotted itself. That's how it goes when your primary concern isn't consequence or acceptance.

Managing the people on that journey with you is important. You can only do that by making them feel like they are part of it. As a leader, it's easy to tell people what to do. And you might be lucky enough that they'll actually do what you say. That will, however, only get you so far. But when you involve them in the journey, in your world, well they're not necessarily going to obsess as you might, or be equally immersed in it, but they can understand how they're contributing. People will accept it and they will feel as though it's something from which they can derive satisfaction. People will feed off the devotion. They will grow into the vision. They will contribute to the greater cause, even if they are seeking other outcomes for themselves. But the sum of the parts will overcome if the leader has envisaged the end point, doesn't deviate from the path to get there, and communicates along the way. People derive strength and purpose from that. I learned that from watching my dad.

My parents' decision to leave Greece was brave. It was courageous. It was non-conformist. It was desperate. To leave home and go to the other side of the world, where we knew nobody, didn't know the language, had no connection to people or place, armed only with the hope of something better. That's quite something. And within that context, even though he'd made the great leap, my father held onto some of the things he'd left behind, including his passion for football.

It was a different time for my dad, growing up. Authority existed automatically. Parents, teachers, police and similar figures had standing. What they said, we did. That doesn't exist as much in today's world. Dad was head of the household and he made the decisions. We didn't need to know why. From that perspective, and with a headstrong sister, I understand why there was tension. It wasn't pleasant but neither do I judge it. That was when I understood that unless everyone is involved in the journey, while you might be able to coerce people, it doesn't make for happiness.

Sitting with Dad at the table with his mates, talking football, that was him including me on the journey. Football was the conduit. I can't remember a discussion with my father about anything other than football. That was it for us. He never gave me advice on girls, or life. It was just football. Even today, that's the conversation. He was a hard man. He was critical of me as a player. I was never good enough. It used to give me the shits. It still does. Even today: 'Look Dad, here's the Asian Cup.'

And what does he say? 'Yeah, but if you made a better substitution you wouldn't have needed extra time.'

'Cheers,' I tell him.

The migrant kids of the Prahran team won the Under 12s state championships. The photo is priceless. We're standing with our pennants and a Supernaut vinyl album as our prize, wearing sleeveless woollen footy jumpers and tight shorts; our state championship uniforms. Me, player/coach, twelve years old. We won it at Middle Park, South Melbourne Hellas's ground. My home away from home.

2

IT DOESN'T DEPEND

Football is the world's most popular game, yet in sports-mad Australia the prevailing feeling is that the sport has struggled to establish a foothold. It's a quandary for me. That assessment is wrong on many levels, but when talking about whether the sport has a place or not in this country one must make the terms of reference very clear. At a participation level, the game not only has an established foothold, but is clearly the dominant sport. None of the other football codes come close to matching football's popularity and, indeed, the combined participation numbers of all three (Aussie Rules, Rugby League and Rugby Union) still fall short of football's.

In 2015 Roy Morgan Research identified football as the most popular game for kids aged between six and thirteen, for the first time surpassing swimming. In that age bracket the football participation rate now sits at 50 per cent. The same data shows girls are now playing football more than they are netball, the hitherto unassailable frontrunner in female sport. So, make no bones about it, football is huge, even in Australia. The challenges confronting football are not in the game's uptake but in turning that grassroots support into a successful commercial product at the professional and elite levels.

There are, I'd say, deep historical and sociological reasons why football has been marginalised over the generations in Australia. As the late Johnny Warren said in his biography, *Sheilas, Wogs and Poofters*, it is more than strange that, as a former British colony, Australia would shun what is by far the most popular sport in Britain. In fact the only places where football isn't the single biggest sport are, like us, former British colonies: the USA, Canada, New Zealand, (white) South Africa, the Subcontinent.

Football's Australian history has, recently at least, mostly been a story of the internal struggles for control of the sport and the external battle for institutional acceptance, or anyway acceptance at the big end of town. The only thing really beyond dispute is that the establishment, some time ago, decided to hitch its wagon to other football codes. Those allegiances have been impenetrable for football for a long time. Those moments when the nexus has been broken, it's been through boldness and courage. Looking through recent history, that's what has changed the paradigm for football. To make its point, football has had to crash through. One can't help but hanker for more of the same.

In anyone's language, moving club football (of any code) from a state-based competition to a national league is a major step, a moment where you either crash or crash through. The first sport to do that in Australia was football, via the National Soccer League, established in 1977. It speaks volumes about the energy and positivity of those involved with the game, and that of the decision-makers. To take such a bold step without the support of the business and political establishments, in contravention of outsiders' view of the game, was truly ground-breaking and inspirational. They knew it was the right thing to do, but there wasn't any really compelling example to copy. At the time neither the AFL nor the NRL were even a twinkle in their forebears' eye. Aussie Rules and Rugby League were so immersed in their Victorian and NSW competitions that they hadn't even considered a national competition.

Unlike the A-League in 2005, when Australia qualified for the 1974 World Cup three years before the formation of the NSL, there was no feel-good over-flow into the domestic game. It had been a singularly momentous achievement, but it did not produce a euphoric, supportive environment. You have to wonder, what made people in football believe they could make something as outrageous as an NSL work? It was an amazingly bold step for the game. And when there *was* euphoria, some thirty years later in the 2006 World Cup finals in Germany, those were the fruits of that bravery. The so-called Golden Generation broke new barriers for football in Australia. It was undoubtedly a long germination period, but the fans and the players had their genesis in the NSL.

The beauty of the NSL was the access and opportunity it gave to many kids. Mark Viduka for example, from the western suburbs of Melbourne and one of our best ever players, was afforded the chance to play on a national stage for his childhood club, Melbourne Croatia. Viduka remembers frequently that his sole ambition as a kid was to play for the Croatian-backed team. After traversing the globe playing football in some of the world's biggest leagues and competitions, as well as captaining Australia in that 2006 World Cup, he remembers most fondly his time as a Melbourne Croatia player. That was his community and Melbourne Croatia was their team. The NSL provided that platform and we benefitted from it via that great Socceroos team in Germany. The doors were opened to many like him. That was the NSL at its grandest. That was the bounty of the bold decision to take the game national. There were no guarantees that it would work and history records, as I've also attempted to record here, that for one reason or another it ground to a halt. But in the meantime it produced amazing things, which by themselves justify the whole journey.

I remember very clearly the great sense of excitement that accompanied the brave new world of the NSL. We seem to think the current A-League epoch is something totally new, but I get more than an occasional sense of déjà vu. I was a ball boy at Middle Park in that first season and some of the crowds that attended were astronomical, certainly compared with the ground's capacity. The NSL brought interstate teams and that created an immense change in attitude. Previously we'd venture across state borders to compete in various cup competitions, but the meat-and-drink emphasis of club football was always local rather than national. The NSL changed that. Its newness and excitement harnessed a lot of energy. Coupled with the grandness of it all was the quirkiness of having Mooroolbark, truly a suburban club from Melbourne's north-east, playing in that inaugural NSL season.

But the NSL started to lose steam because at some point there was a feeling that it wasn't sustainable any longer. The people who had initially driven and financed the game weren't seeing a return. Their response was to cut costs and scale things back. The media exposure began to lessen. After beginning life with a naming-rights sponsor, as the Philips Soccer League, and being telecast on the Ten Network, the game migrated to public broadcasters, eventually finding its way to the somewhat niche SBS. That entrenched a common and convenient view that football was other, niche and foreign. SBS was football's proper place, comparatively out of sight and out of mind. Of course denying the huge impact the network played over years in exposing youngsters to international football would be ludicrous. Johnny Warren labelled SBS 'Australia's best coach' and, for the period of SBS's primacy, that resonates with me deeply.

As the media landscape changed, other competition ideas to enliven the NSL were considered. Some worked and some didn't. The competition was split into two conferences, the aim of which was to simultaneously increase the number of teams, adding to the league's political power-base as a faction inside the national governing body, and to reduce the costs of interstate travel incurred by clubs. Clearly this decision to con-solidate, both financially and politically, diluted the value of a national competition. A system of promotion and relegation was also implemented, but again the mechanics proved problematic and soon became overly political. In hindsight these decisions were whimsical and their lack of planning added to the league's downward spiral. A series of problematic decisions rolled off the production line without any coordination; let's try this, let's try that. There was no common belief or direction pulling the NSL through its plateaus.

The last big moment of note for the NSL was the move, in 1989, to playing the season in the summer. It proved an idea of such substance that it's still a fundamental plank in the A-League. So profound was that decision's success that when the A-League hit the road there wasn't, as far as I can recall, any talk at all of the competition not being played in summer. In 1989 it was not just moving the NSL season but an entire football code from winter to summer – a huge conceptual undertaking, but one that has passed the test of time. It's probably true that as an idea it operated outside any formal strategic framework, but nevertheless it worked. The relatively uncontested media landscape over the summer period and the more pleasant conditions for fans were the two big reasons for its undertaking. Moving the season also gave the NSL greater alignment with European football, which remains an important consideration with regard to transfers and international fixtures. Playing conditions were also a consideration, because the warmer months meant better-grassed fields on which to play. Access to stadiums, however, wasn't a big factor in those early days as most of the clubs played at their suburban grounds, as opposed to using municipal stadiums as the A-League clubs do (and which presents myriad headaches now).

The point about summer football and its introduction was that somebody in charge thought outside the square and realised the need to break away, seeing no purpose in doing what everyone did just because that's what had always been done. The decision was taken because it was better for the competition and for the sport.

However, despite the ballsy decisions to go national and play in summer, conservatism and self-doubt grew within the game's administration. The emphasis swung toward consolidation, minimisation and being happy to fit only into the space afforded to the sport. Ultimately the niche-bubble, which felt comfortable for some inside the game, extinguished the NSL. The oxygen just ran out.

The majority of the NSL clubs were ethnic in profile. That is widely held as the reason for the competition's demise. This was actually the strength of the game when it started, guaranteeing many clubs consistently big crowds. In general, the clubs failed over time to address the changing status of their own members and fans. The clubs needed to move to ensure the bond between club and fan remained strong. It was a singular weakness of NSL clubs that they failed in this.

A good example from my own observations was South Melbourne. South moved from Middle Park to their new home, Bob Jane Stadium at Albert Park, where they still play today. This occurred purely as a consequence of the government taking over Middle Park for the Formula One racing track. The first game at the new venue attracted 15 000 people. This was a walk-up crowd, there was no promotion or advertising. People just came. The new facility was the major draw-card. Of course there was some novelty value, but the fact that people could sit in seats and not on wooden benches felt life-changing. Traditional South supporters had grown up with poor facilities as the status quo. The new venue showed how well people responded to modern service and comfort. But South failed to realise this was something tap into, there wasn't sufficient understanding of the need to appeal to families. Time passed and nothing was done with this new venue, it gradually lost its sheen and the crowds dropped again. Keeping things the way they'd been for twenty years proved to be a recipe for failure. Facilities and toilets weren't comfortable, there was a lack of diversity in food outlets and other basics were more or less ignored. As the expectations of supporters changed, South remained in a time warp. And they weren't alone.

To me, that wasn't about identity or stubbornness or exclusiveness. It was about keeping up with modern sport. NSL clubs could have done that without losing their identity. Making a Greek or Croatian or Italian club more appealing to people not from that background may have taken a bit of thought, but it wouldn't have been impossible if there had been a will to do so. The clubs missed the boat by not opening their doors further. In their defence, the clubs were operating without any real directive or clear leadership on these matters. They were working in isolation to find solutions. And if one club took a progressive stance on an issue they'd soon play a club that was more recalcitrant, and progress would stall. Football was growing exponentially but there were few places for the new players and fans to congregate, to form attachments to clubs that were relevant to them and their expectations. These were testing times that needed a coordinated approach. When it wasn't forthcoming, the NSL increasingly became an outcast in its own sport.

Much of the decision-making was reactionary. Ultimately we're talking about clubs that were moving towards professionalism on the field, with players of considerable worth on the international transfer market in their ranks, but off the field they were being run by a staff of one or two full-time employees. The bulk of the slack was picked up by volunteers. In essence these were community clubs operating beneath a veneer of professionalism. It was very difficult, if not impossible, to expect the game to keep pace with professional administrations when the NSL and its clubs weren't investing in those types of resources. The NSL was started by people of vision and passion and it seemed over time, and particularly towards the end, they were replaced by people of convenience.

There was definitely a feeling at the time that there was an anti-football agenda being pursued by elements of the media. And it's hard to deny the landscape as it was. People with vested interests were threatened by football and their objections to the game were loud and frequent. There were plenty of occasions where the accusations being levelled weren't of any great substance, but that mattered neither to those prosecuting the case nor those consuming the message. It was a significant combination to overcome, and the sport itself played into it with its overt politicisation and amateurish handling of those issues.

The media atmosphere had an influence on the NSL's decline, but it's folly to put all the blame at its feet. It was football's job to rise above all that and create such a compelling case that dissension would have eventually subsided. Of course that was possible, but it could only have been achieved with a laser focus and commitment to game-growing initiatives. The fact that football withdrew into a political morass and became organisationally dysfunctional is not necessarily the fault of a hostile media, even if they were delighted by that and reported it enthusiastically. Too enthusiastically at times, and in the absence of any balanced coverage of the football itself. The game could never be the story, only the controversies around it; that's something that has frustrated football followers for years, I guess. Still, if that was the challenge for football to overcome, it should have and could have done so.

Instead, the NSL just lost its way. There ceased to be any new or forward thinking. Expansion into new territories was resisted, if it happened at all. Again, the politics became so survivalist and introspective that the game's growth was running a distant second. That it took until 1996 to install Perth Glory into the NSL reflects this, particularly as the Glory quickly became the club pointing everyone to the future. If other clubs had tried to emulate then Glory chairman Nick Tana, perhaps the NSL may have survived in its own right.

Another key to the stagnation was the repeated failure to qualify for the World Cup. These attempts famously became a quadrennial cycle of heartbreak. The lack of international participation crippled football's path to acceptance. Australians love winners. Adulation for any athletes and teams who win on the international stage is readily forthcoming from the Australian populace. The fact that much of that joy has historically been derived by winning relatively small competitions, including some sports at the Olympics, isn't something processed by our country. It's why, I guess, we still get into a lather about winning Commonwealth Games gold medals in swimming for example – truckloads of them! – despite the fact that large chunks of the Commonwealth don't, for all intents and purposes, swim. The Australian sports fan doesn't always exhibit a keen sense of perspective on these matters. Perhaps we might label ourselves flat-track bullies? Football fans on the other hand understand intimately that serious international competition – such as in the world of football – is a very difficult thing at which to succeed. Without the appropriate filters domestically, Australian football's lack of international success dovetailed with the prevailing sentiment that football was inadequate and un-Australian. It has been a difficult stigma for football to shake; the NSL proved incapable of dealing with that burden.

So the NSL was left to live or die under its own steam.

It got no help from any sort of successful or vibrant international match program. It was tethered to existing, bomb-proof governance structures that were resistant to progress, vigorously defended, and time and again proved incompatible with releasing the game into its potential. Eventually the forces against the NSL became too much. The writing had been on the wall for some time and there was a sense of inevitability about the demise.

The clubs themselves were gradually becoming less relevant. Their importance as a social outlet for people lessened over time, for differing reasons. There was certainly not the reliance on them for the bedrock of social contact as had once been the case, and so people became disengaged with the football side of things too. The quality of the game, and the lack of exposure, meant that the market the NSL started with in 1977 was basically the only one it reached until its death in 2004. Not even the inclusion of new clubs, such as Northern Spirit, Carlton or Parramatta Power could save the competition.

Prior to those clubs joining, the NSL did make attempts at broadening its base – by Australianising. South Melbourne became Gunners and Lakers rather than Hellas. There were Stallions, Warriors, Zebras, Sharks, Pride (if you can believe that), Knights and other sobriquets that were meant to alter the tone of the league. But nothing except the nomenclature changed so it was literally only cosmetic. Clubs continued as they were, operating in a governance system that was congenitally dysfunctional. The name changes actually fuelled the feeling that the game itself wasn't good enough and needed Australianising to work. The bizarre paradox, as it appeared to me, was the re-naming of clubs smacked more of Americanisation than anything. It seems ridiculous now that anyone thought changing names and nothing else would be enough, but that's as far as any changes really went.

One of the bigger implications for football was the fact that other codes emerged from the semi-professional era more quickly. Aussie Rules and, to a lesser extent, Rugby League began to administer their sports more professionally and act more strategically. Meanwhile, people were trying to make football more appealing without properly coming to grips with the business of sport. The NSL's future may have been brighter if there were more professional people involved in setting its strategic direction. This was something new to Australia as a whole, not just football. When Australia was beginning to wake up to the fact that sport is not just a pastime but actually a profession, football was tightly snuggled-up in its doona, dozing through the earliest hours of the new dawn. It's been playing catch-up ever since.

———

Bold moves can lose momentum because in the face of inevitable struggle, people weaken. The NSL and the move to summer were great things. But by themselves they were never going to deliver the promised land. There were always going to be struggles and too many in football shy away from the struggle. In part because they can't see through to the other side, which is made worse by a lack of clarity, understanding and leadership.

But people also want easy answers. We see other sports on easy street and can't understand why we can't have that too. It's understandable to a point, but in any walk of life, if easy street isn't the reality, you've got to strive to change the circumstances. The struggle is the important bit as far as I'm concerned; it fortifies you, makes the vision absolutely clear. Too often in football we don't seem prepared to take that on, or at least not often enough. We change tack when the waters get a bit choppy. Whenever there's an issue in the game, for example, we get defensive and blame the media. It's an unwelcome, unhealthy and unfulfilling cycle. We lose focus, we stop moving forward, we begin to question and then we second-guess.

I think the A-League is now courting a similar cycle to the NSL, albeit with a lot more money at its disposal and plenty more exposure. We're hearing a lot about consolidation and sustainability. Once you get into consolidation mode the next step is trying to minimise loss, and shrinkage soon follows. I think that's the juncture the A-League is at now. It needs to take more bold steps if it really wants to be the league we all believed it could be – although what exactly that looks like remains a bit hazy. From my vantage point, I'm not sure the envisioned end point has actually been declared.

This would be one of the major things I'd address. There has to be a unified view on what the league looks like when it's matured. And that position has to be made very public, to give people the chance to get excited and work towards that outcome. In my mind we'd be able to look to every corner of the country and see an opportunity for a kid to play football for a team that represents them. If we achieve that, the game will never look back. We have more kids playing this year than we did last, and that trend will continue. Football can't be stopped. Consolidating at a time of growth seems counterintuitive to me. We should be right in the middle of an investment boom.

I gather people are nervous about stating the competition's aims publicly, presuming such a thing has even been quantified somewhere. My view is that we should be loud and proud about where we and the league are headed, and then let's go for it. Once you start consolidating you start being exclusive. That was the catchcry of those explaining away the death of the NSL: that it was excluding people. We shouldn't wantonly repeat such an error. We have a special opportunity. The numbers don't lie and the international opportunities, particularly through Asia, are going to grow immensely. So if the game is struggling to fund itself, sell the story to partners who can invest. If Australian football is to become more accessible to all those who love the game, the answer isn't to repeat the mistakes of twenty years ago.

The 2015 FFA Cup final was, for me, a classic example. A tournament open to teams throughout Australian football, not just the A-League clubs, is a great concept. I do wonder why it took until 2014 to come to life but it's here now and has been very well received. But we get to the 2015 final and a question confronts the organisers: what's more important, money in the bank or the opportunity to sell out a stadium and make a statement with this fledgling competition? Are tickets priced to fill the venue with 30 000 people or are the prices ramped up to try and fill a hole in the balance sheet? Deciding in favour of the balance sheet is consolidation, not a growth strategy. I firmly believe we should be investing in the game's opportunities. Money is not always the answer; often the idea comes before the money. According to Tim Cook, CEO of Apple, the company chases great products, not money. The money follows the great products. Apple seems to be doing fine.

The A-League is a great product but it can't be what Australia needs it to be with just ten teams. It's like saying I've got ten stores but next year I'm going to have a million new customers, many of them will be in areas where I don't have stores but I'll still try to service them with the existing set-up. It doesn't make sense. It may be enough for a financial model in a boardroom but it's out of whack with the reality of the opportunity. The huge opportunity football offers is what's going to fill the gap in the balance sheet, not juggling around line-items on a budget.

Part of the success of the NSL was the ability to have two teams in a city like Adelaide, both generating significant interest. The same for Sydney and Melbourne and Brisbane. More teams generated more talk and analysis and interest. People had a choice of teams to follow. We're not at that point yet in the A-League, but I'd be getting there as fast as I could. I'd be breaking doors down to make it happen. Local derbies are good for the fans and good for the clubs rising to meet those competitive challenges. People can talk and talk about the relative sizes of cities and so on, but you only have to look at how, since their addition to the league in 2012, the Western Sydney Wanderers have pushed A-League incumbents Sydney FC to improve their operations. Competition does that. For so long Sydney FC, and others, resisted expansion in that city until everyone felt Sydney FC was stable enough and ready for it. But left to themselves some clubs will never be ready. So what do we do, never expand? The truth is that competition expedited that development of Sydney FC's 'metrics'. That was the impact of the Wanderers, in that city alone. Now imagine the A-League as a whole without the impact of the Wanderers.

Of course the Western Sydney Wanderers are a massive success story. And the formation of that club is another example of football being bold. I am at a bit of a loss as to why the Wanderers experience doesn't provide the game with more energy to push the boundaries. The rhetoric is that Sydney's west was ready for action and it's hard to find other places similarly primed. But, if the western suburbs of Sydney were such an obvious market, why wasn't the A-League there from day one? And it is a tad disingenuous to pump out a line that western Sydney was just ready to go but other areas aren't. Before the Wanderers, Football Federation Australia had issued an exclusive opportunity to Sydney Rovers to become the licence holder for Sydney's west. They were to be the vanguard of A-League expansion into that football hotbed. After the period of exclusivity, the Rovers' board reported back to the FFA that they couldn't find the capital to get the club started, or operational, or sustainable.

The idea of expanding into a second Sydney team was put back in the cupboard. That is fact, not revisionism.

The circumstances that brought about the decision to start the Wanderers were encased in deep turmoil, with the cancellation of Gold Coast United's A-League licence and the spat between its owner Clive Palmer and the FFA. It must be remembered that the Wanderers were put together in extreme haste out of the need to fill a ten-team competition schedule, not because an irrefutable business case had been made.

Faced with this reality – necessity being the mother of invention and all that – the FFA created the Western Sydney Wanderers in next to no time. It was a ridiculously short lead-in. Coach Tony Popovic put a team together in three months. He has gone on to reach amazing heights in just a matter of years. The FFA administered the club through the period of its foundation and did an amazing job. The community consultation that was undertaken should be a pointer as to how things should be done in the future and the incredible results that it can bring. Truly, I can't for the life of me understand why the Wanderers exercise doesn't fire up our game to be bolder with its expansion plans. I give no credence to the line that there are no other areas like western Sydney. The Rovers exercise told us western Sydney wasn't ready and look how wrong that proved to be. For whatever reason we continue to view opportunities as we did with Rovers, rather than being emboldened by the Wanderers.

While I firmly believe league expansion should be a central discussion, it must be said that the initial concept of one team per city, almost like state of origin, worked. The parameters were set out very clearly and it was a success. It's always easier to build something when the vision is clear and, to me, the initial drive behind the A-League was very clear. But we quickly realised the eight teams weren't enough. From there we've gone from having a very clear outline, to realising we'd outgrown that, but then never replacing that original incarnation with a clear new vision. There's haziness around the league, it confuses people and therefore fails to enlist them to the cause.

We should be striving for a competitive season (that includes FFA Cup, Asian Champions League, maybe breaks for FIFA's international match windows) that runs from August or September to May. There should be derbies in each state. We should be aiming for a thirty-game season with a fifteen- to sixteen-team competition. Plus finals. The clubs would then be heading towards the forty games per season mark. That then becomes comparable to other leagues around the world. We don't target the overseas leagues as a benchmark because we need them for validation, we target them because this is our competition and we concede an advantage by not matching the optimum quantity of games.

I believe there should also be a move towards owning our own stadiums. Certainly we need purpose-built stadiums. We see other countries building facilities with less space and bigger populations, but they seem to be able do it. We say we don't have the space or the money. If I was a Western Sydney Wanderer I'd say let's build our own venue. Why not? Why can't it be done? If we believe the game is going to be as big as we say, then it will have to have its own stadiums to satisfy the demands of fans and match schedules. And in order for it to become that big, owning our own stadiums is the only means of delivery.

Our views on what makes a club also need massaging. Clubs must belong to their communities if they're going to work. Real success will come when they do belong to communities. Many owners, including really successful businessmen, have been brought to their knees by fans saying, 'No, this isn't yours, and we're not supporting it or relating to the way you're running it.' We have this notion, currently, that clubs are run by individuals. But look at Melbourne Victory, the best model in the league – you never hear about the owners of the club. It's a private venture but they reinvest all profits back into the club. No one personality controls it and, for the most part, it belongs to the fans. The Wanderers were born out of the same thing. Fans were asked what their team should be called, what they should wear, where they should play. The opposite end of that spectrum is the rogue owner, of whom there have been too many in the league. Look at the disaster of Nathan Tinkler's reign in Newcastle; no connection with the fans or the community so the club was run as he saw fit. Same with Clive Palmer on the Gold Coast, look at where they ended up. The results were disastrous. Business people can't seem to separate their normal transactions with what it means to take control of a sporting club. They see it as another acquisition. It's not that. They are really just custodians of a public property, even if it is their money propping up the licence. In reality they are paying for the privilege of custodianship, not ownership. Clubs will always be owned by their supporters. Smart people understand that community is what makes A-League clubs work. There haven't been enough smart people at A-League clubs.

Certainly the ownership model remains under scrutiny. The safe option is just to distribute licences based on bank balance; a strategy that chases capital rather than finding the best person for the job. The due diligence processes have, in some cases at least, left a lot to be desired. Perhaps the next bold step will be for the FFA to resist the easy option of another rich fat cat to pay the bills and instead moving towards a model that formalises communities as stakeholders of their clubs. The driving force behind the decisions of management must be what is good for the game long-term. Money will follow that commitment.

Fans won't respect an owner purely because he or she has money. Just take a look at the wealth behind the American owners of England's Liverpool FC. They saunter into town echoing emptiness about doing something for the fans of Liverpool, then they jack up ticket prices. It's not lost on the fans, many of whom come from working-class families, that the owners are billionaires already. So when they ramped up ticket prices, 10 000 Liverpool fans walked out in protest in the seventy-seventh minute of a home game in February 2016. It was the first time in the 124-year history of the club that fans had staged a walkout. If you're the owner, you realise you can't just do what you want, even if you do own the club. All your money is worth-less if you've ignored the community. As Professional Footballers Australia proclaimed in its Australian Premier League competition proposal (launched as a replacement for the NSL): No fans no value. Not every rich owner of a football club makes that connection. One buys a sporting club to be part of something, the good owners understand that.

———

Football seems to be in an introspective mode at the moment. We're head down, dealing with today's problems. The problem with these periods is that you lose sight of the horizon and inertia sets in. There's no clearly articulated plan for how we are going to get to the light on the hill. Football people can see that place, can imagine what it's like to get there, yet the brakes are on. The game itself is turbocharged but the rhetoric and vision are coming via carrier pigeon. There is an imbalance and a disconnect; the game is in the enviable position of having a huge presence and participation rate but it doesn't have a story to leverage that huge presence. To me, the story very clearly is that the game is waiting to boom and waiting for the leaders to take it, us, into that land of milk and honey. What are we waiting for? Let's get it done. People will respond if you're bold and courageous. Conversely, they'll leave you to wither if you lack the courage required for their game. They believe in it – do you? They want you to drive hard – will you?

What the football community gets instead are repeated helpings of 'it depends'. Football can't actualise anything with 'depends' leadership. The NSL going national, the move to summer, the instalment of the A-League, moving to the Asian Confederation, establishing the Western Sydney Wanderers and the inauguration of the FFA Cup weren't 'depends' leadership and management moments.

Under current criteria, there was no justification for any of them, really. But they were decisions that were made because it was what the game needed, and it worked. We need more of that. If I ran my dressing room as a 'depends' coach I'd be a castaway. It doesn't depend. You have to take control and make it happen. That's the story of my coaching. That's the story that the game will tell when it has reached its summit, a point that will only be reached if we're bold and courageous.

3

LEGACIES

I am a competitive person. Outthinking, outsmarting, outflanking, outplaying my opponents is what I seek to do in football. I don't like to lose. I hate it, in fact. Losing makes me grumpy. The best measure of the effectiveness of my strategies, over time, is how often my team and I win. For that reason the scoreboard is useful. But I don't light incense at its altar, genuflect to it, deify it. It's a tool but it's not my reason for existing. It just so happens that, if I've done what I've set out to do, the scoreboard has usually acceded. Scores and tables will change like weather systems, areas of high pressure will replace areas of low pressure, a pattern will develop and a season will result. But it will change again, inevitably. Winning is never enough. For me the pursuit of winning and trophies without attaching any meaning to what you're doing is like chasing the wind.

The success of our Prahran High School team was very significant for us. There can be no doubt that part of what drove us was that it wasn't just about football. In the cut-off woollen Aussie Rules jumpers that weighed a ton when it rained (and remember, it's Melbourne winter we're talking about) and the almost castratingly tight footy shorts, we wanted to show that we were important to the school, not just a sideshow or, worse, an embarrassment. We pushed hard believing that the following year the school would get us our own playing strip, a proper football one, and afford us some measure of status. Winning games helped our cause and raised our profile but to win wasn't the end of our ambition. Even as a young coach I was already programmed by the subtleties of my upbringing, the battle with assimilation. My recollections are that race relations were pretty raw back then and we had a point to prove. That gave us extra impetus and made every win more poignant.

It needs to be appreciated that Australia, at the time, hadn't really come to terms with multiculturalism. It was government policy but it wasn't really community practice. And my cohort was really in the first wave of migrant kids, or thereabouts, at our particular school. Families like mine, whose time was spent in the Greek community and at South Melbourne Hellas, were pretty easily ignored by the wider society. No one really wanted to know us. We were a foreign-language-speaking, alternative-cuisine-eating oddity. It was little more than tokenism that our team could be included in a formal competition for a sport that was estranged from the establishment. We were only twelve years old and mightn't really have been attuned to the sociology of the period. Yet as I look back, to be so young and so driven by this particular issue speaks in part to how special that group was, but also to how acute an issue ethnicity and football's place in Australia was at the time. Other schools were, it seemed to us, more invested. For a start they had proper football gear. We weren't out to change the world, but we had something to say about our place in it and our feet would do the talking. Rather than confront the indifference of our school we decided to embrace it all as some sort of badge of honour. I made sure that was drummed into all of us. We were going to show everyone. I recall saying they might be laughing at us now – and we did look totally ridiculous lining up in the pre-loved Aussie Rules gear – but who'll be laughing at the end? Our purpose was more than results; results were how we made our point.

———

If I look at the clubs and places I've coached, meaning has always been the most important ingredient for the journey. My playing career hasn't shaped my coaching too much. Many players enter coaching on the back of exultant achievements and their coaching is an extension of that. It's very different for me. My playing career was a frustration. The limits of my ability meant that I was restricted in what I could control. As a result, I don't think I enjoyed playing as much as I should have. I was always a coach masquerading as a player, really. People often come up and say that nothing must beat the experience of playing, but for me, coaching does. And the cornerstone for that was my experience with Prahran.

My home club, though, is South Melbourne Hellas. It's the only club I ever played for (other than the school team). My playing days ended unceremoniously in 1993, when I was only twenty-seven. I remained at the club, however, and when I was thirty I became South's head coach. As with my ascension to the Prahran job, moving into the position at Hellas seemed completely normal to me. Others were surprised because I was young and inexperienced, but coaching South Melbourne was something that I was always going to do. My conviction didn't waver when I took the reins of a dressing room that was full of great players, many of whom were internationals, some of whom were older than me, and a few of whom were very close friends. Others expected all this to be difficult and strange. I don't recall even blinking at the prospect.

It was very important that even for this first posting I didn't position myself as someone who'd transitioned from player to coach simply because I didn't have anything else to do. Plenty of coaches end up in the job for that precise reason: an absence of any alternative pursuit. To me, that is like spending a lifetime walking around in shoes that are two sizes too small. I can't comprehend why people would do it. Those coaches' players, inevitably, sense the discomfort and vacuums are created. At that point the coach has even more difficult work to do and in an environment that was already uncomfortable for them to begin with.

I didn't start as Hellas coach from that trajectory. Having been a 'lifer' at South, I was deeply inculcated with the club's ways. I had a deep appreciation of where the club was and what it had been. I was deeply indebted to the club for the role it had played in the life of my family. As head coach, I knew exactly what I wanted to achieve there.

There may have been an expectation that I'd slip into the coaching job, hit autopilot and churn out the same training sessions, team talks and tactics that I'd experienced as a player. Plenty of ex-players fall into that and there was no way I was going to be that type of coach. I wasn't going to slouch into that first job, ease my way in, fumble my way through. I was going to hit the ground running. I was going to put the club and everyone involved on notice. I was going to shake the place up. South Melbourne, it seemed to me, suffered from a type of lethargy. There was a softness in the club. It would rise to the top and immediately fall back to mediocrity. I wasn't going to be part of that.

For me, South Melbourne Hellas had to be great. In the NSL South had been a winning team, but I don't think it could say it was a great club. It was a big club with a great history, many fans and a large profile, but it wasn't great. For it to be great, in my mind, it had to build a dynasty. Having been there since I was nine years old, and being part of the post-game discussions with my dad and his mates, it just didn't compute with me that the winning record had remained so patchy. Great clubs don't win inconsistently. They dominate. As South had in the pre-NSL days.

I could sense from early on that people presumed I'd be looking for a cushy existence, happy to be part of the furniture. That summed up to me why the club was where it was. I inherited a very good team, one that would have had a chance of winning without a coach at all. But I didn't just want to win and secure my tenure that way. I had played two hundred games for the club over nine senior years and won two championships, the second as captain of the club. Winning the league as a coach would have consolidated my position there, if that's all I'd wanted. But I think there is something more valuable in doing things that people want to talk about long after you're gone. Maybe that's not important to some people, but it is to me.

I wasn't remotely interested in dancing the win-games-keep-job cha-cha. I wanted to do something special with this team and for this club, something that hadn't been done before. The dream at South was to be the first team to win back-to-back titles.

It was difficult for some people to understand that the initial championship, secured in just my second year of coaching, wasn't enough to calm me down a bit. From the beginning of the NSL, it had taken the club seven years to win its first title in 1984. There was a sense of expectation, if not entitlement, that success would just roll on from there. It wasn't until 1991, another seven years, that the next championship was won. This was one of the biggest clubs in the country yet success was sporadic. It was a club with a seven-year itch that I needed to scratch.

I made sure that I drove everyone at the club hard from the moment the curtain fell on that first success in 1998. There would be no let-up. Some friction was caused because people wanted me to calm down. After all, what could I be worried about? With a title under my belt, I was safe for life. I very keenly felt the pressure to relax. But I also recognised the sense of back to the future. I'd been at South for twenty-five years and seen all the ups and downs. I'd experienced the introspection and shared the euphoria. Hellas's version of great was at odds with the world greats of my childhood, who I'd come to know as I read football magazines as a kid. How could my great Hellas not have the same greatness as Manchester United or Liverpool or Barcelona or Ajax Amsterdam or Bayern Munich? They always won. Relentlessly. My Hellas, in whom I'd invested so much and from whom my family and community had gotten even more back, bobbed around like a cork on the ocean. I'd wallow in my own sort of cognitive dissonance; those greats versus Hellas's version of great.

There was only one option, then. For South Melbourne Hellas to wear the same halo as the world's most famous clubs, it had to expunge the inconsistency. My team was going to set that straight. As coach I would talk about the club's great players, its great history, its deep importance to the Greek community. I kept on about the opportunity at hand, about how big the club could become and how right that would be. I wanted to make Hellas an unstoppable force, which meant that winning that first title didn't really excite me. It merely set the scene for the main act, the title defence the next season.

I had to ensure that the board was part of this too. I was constantly exhorting them to strive for diligence and excellence, to not let the grass grow under their feet or get distracted by league or club politics. Nobody at South wanted the team to be fly-by-nights but, until now, there hadn't been a plan or a person to do anything about it. With the board I made sure that the whole club was sharpened to this focus. We made sure that there wasn't a huge turnover of players and that key individuals were secured. NSL clubs typically had revolving-door policies on player recruitment and retention. Hellas couldn't be like that if we were going to change the paradigm, so the board got supportive and active in retaining the players we needed. We brought in the two or three players we needed to strengthen. I had to pester people to get the outcomes we needed. It got to the point where people would duck into a spare room if they saw me approaching in a corridor. They thought I wasn't noticing, but I was. All the while I was figuring out who could be included in this journey, who could be relied upon when things got sticky. People who'd jump at my shadow wouldn't last long. I wasn't out to get rid of them, at least not directly, but they wouldn't be able to take the heat and I was about to turn up the dial.

The most important part of this was to be able to look captain Paul Trimboli in the eye, as well as all the other players who'd already achieved success, and have them believe when I said to them, 'This is your chance to do something that's permanent.' This was their chance at making history.

It was imperative that everyone saw that I acted as I spoke. There was no complacency from me. In fact, into the title defence, I became more edgy, more defined. I walked into the pre-season training sessions knowing that the players' antennae were up. *How fair dinkum is he going to be?* If I didn't hit that mark then, right from the outset, I'd have lost them. There couldn't be a single moment of laxness. Not a hint of easing back into rhythm. My demeanour, my language, my glare and my expectations all needed to go up a notch from the season before. I had to change training, I brought in a Brazilian coach for a spell. I had to challenge them more.

I kept the players on their toes. I had to make them understand that we were starting from zero again. Winning the previous season doesn't give any advantage going into the next. That's the thing about winning. It comes, it goes. It won't carry you into or through the next campaign. You have to start again. You have to find the reason to start again. Climbing Everest suc-cessfully once doesn't mean that the next time you start automatically closer to the summit. Every successful ascent begins in the same place, base camp.

Most people who get to climb Everest do it once and that's it. Because while the view from the top is fantastic, they know exactly what they spent getting up there and don't want to do it again. Or, if they like the thought of reaching it again, they aren't actually prepared to do what is required. For most, they've seen it once and that's enough. And that's fair enough. But my mission was to climb that mountain again, right there and then. There wasn't going to be a season-long rest, enjoying that first title for a year before having another tilt. Hellas were going to go hell-for-leather for consecutive titles. Now that would be something. We were going up that mountain again and only those prepared for what that meant would remain. I had to set those boundaries and expectations very clearly, and early. This would be a test for us all because doing it back to back was uncharted territory. And in making clear my aims and ambitions, I was sticking my neck out.

I had to convince the players that it could be done and that in fact they wanted to do it. You know the view will be the same. You know the air will be as rarefied. You know you'll get the same reward. You know it's going to hurt to get there. But you also know you'll be the first to have done it. Now, that's something.

We climbed Everest that next season. Consecutive

NSL titles for the first time in the club's history. The reward was to represent the Oceania Confederation in the FIFA Club World Cup. This, for me, was where South Melbourne were meant to be. This was the appropriate stage. The club champions of all of FIFA's six confederations in the one place, vying for world club champion status. The tournament was held in Rio de Janeiro and we were grouped with Manchester United and Vasco da Gama (a huge Brazilian club based in Rio). With the same energy and drive, we tackled two of the world's most famous clubs, playing in arguably the world's most famous stadium, the Maracanã in Rio. The same stadium where an estimated 200 000 spectators watched Uruguay defeat Brazil to win the 1950 World Cup; the competition's biggest-ever upset. Could South Melbourne Hellas perform their own miracle there? These were the stories and places South Melbourne needed to be a part of. This was where I wanted to take my club.

We didn't win, but we performed with credit and showed we were not out of place in those surroundings. As happens in football, there were two or three golden moments that could have turned our performances into stunning upsets, but it wasn't to be. We didn't win, but we'd found meaning.

———

Legacy is important because it gives those who come after opportunities to set new marks, create new end points, live new adventures. That's how growth happens. If we remain satisfied with the norm then boundaries aren't extended and we're not pushing for excellence. If a club wins two games in a row it immediately means that, for the next person, three consecutive wins is the target. It forces them to build a framework and sell the story to a new group of people to make their own mark. With this sort of impetus, football moves from being a mere assembly line into a dynamic force that grows beyond its wildest imagining. This sort of competitive drive gets people constantly looking up for new targets, rather than looking sideways to see what everyone else is doing. The difference between working with 'up' energy rather than 'sideways' energy is, I think, obvious. I certainly know which I prefer. It's a slight paradox in me, I guess, because I am compliant by nature. But in football it's different; its grip on me is so entwined with the rest of my character and life. In football I can't settle. With football there is so much still to see.

Ambition based on legacy has always attracted me. It's assumed greater importance for me because the football market in Australia isn't fully matured and there is so much work still to do, so much possibility. I find myself really responding to people who want to make a difference; I want to make a difference. I get excited and motivated by seeing others trying to extend the reach of football. I accept the mindset is different in sports where the market is matured. Where the path is really well worn and the frontier bested, the focus then does become the dichotomy of winning and losing.

In football, legacy is taking the world I've imagined and making it real for other people. When in a role, everything I do is to give life to that world. Individuals involved in that might be driven by conceit – how good it will make them look or how much they'll be rewarded – but that's okay, because the leader has to massage the individual motivations to get people to contribute to the whole. I have big plans for the game in Australia. I have huge faith in it. I know the opportunities are almost boundless. So everything I do as a coach, with the teams that I have, is feeding into that world.

By the time I'd arrived at Brisbane in 2009, halfway through the season, I'd been out of senior coaching for a period, having missed the boat when the A-League set sail in 2005. I'd spent the time in between looking carefully at what had, and hadn't, developed in the local scene. My first thought when I took over Brisbane was not to win the championship, although being a competitive person it was folly for me to deny myself that motivation. But truly, it wasn't about assembling a team to win. What I wanted to do with Brisbane was to change the way football was played in the A-League. With Brisbane I – we – had to do it differently. I felt the league was beset by a mindset of mediocrity. That qualifying for the finals by scraping into sixth, in a ten-team league, could somehow be seen as a success. There was nothing revolutionary, no one was taking a break-away approach. I felt there were enormous operational gaps in the competition and a particularly cavernous lack of ambition. No one was looking for the summit.

The Brisbane exercise needed every single person at the club to buy in, to want to be part of a revolution. It's a pretty intoxicating thing, when the message and plan are so new. And when people can start to see the plan unfolding, and working, they believe even more and put even more in. The binding becomes even stronger. It unleashes enormous energy and endeavour; sometimes, often, it can be quite irresistible. When the dust settled, the scoreboards were taken down and everyone had moved on, there was to remain this team that everyone still talks about. Brisbane were going beyond the scoreboard. We were going to change club football in Australia.

Of course it's a challenge walking into a place and putting something unconventional on the table. People don't like change. Universal acceptance and understanding are never totally forthcoming and yet I've found that, when I've tapped into the right source, the objections have been very few. Even those who have some resistance at first will eventually buy into the project. Most people don't want to find themselves outside the group or its momentum. Getting the group to the point where there is some momentum is the big challenge, and that's the bit I love. I start with the premise that everyone wants to be involved. Everyone must find their place or for them it's going to be a battle. Pitching it so that the majority comes on board is the key.

I honestly start this process with such a total belief in the project that I just assume everyone is going to want to be part of it. In reality that won't be the case, and it's equally true that not everyone in the room at the start will turn out to be my kind of player. Those things work themselves out in their own time.

The bigger the change the bigger the resistance. People don't like to have their comfort zone challenged. But I can't work in a comfort zone. That's not how exciting things are done, as far as I'm concerned. The more I disturb the comfort, the greater the pushback. It becomes very testing when pushback becomes blowback. That can be a make or break time. I'm not a coach for everyone. I'm not a coach for every situation. I'm willing to accommodate people to a certain extent but I'll never abide anything that will derail the mission. The range of personalities and motivations and abilities is so wide that my message and methods just will not resonate with some people. There's no shame in that. I'm still going to push on.

Once I've got the majority of the organisation (club or team) over the momentum tipping point, we're usually away. To get to that point requires inclusiveness; making people believe in what you're doing and feel as though their contribution is vital to its success. No person is more important than another. Any person can be called upon to perform a function and they need to believe that role is key. Even players who aren't regularly playing must feel like they're contributing. From day one I create the story and beat the drum. And, importantly, that first message is never about winning games. That's not different from what people are used to, that's expected. Every coach goes in with that aim. But if that's the level of the ambition and there is no further context or meaning built around it, there is nothing special.

I realise that I ask a lot of people around me, and was doing so at Brisbane. The time was right for both the club and for me to take that path. To change. Change is inconvenient by nature and that was attractive to me because convenience is a soul destroyer. I can't work effectively in that environment, can't get what I need out of coaching. I can't compromise the essence of my coaching – which goes to the heart of me as a person – and settle for a place where I'm just working for the sake of it. That position would trash everything I believe in and keep telling people, and would trample over the coaching achievements I've enjoyed. It isn't always easy, but I see it as a matter of being. Anything less cheapens everything I've done, and want to do, in my life.

At Brisbane I wanted to show that Australian players can adopt an international best-practice playing style, and do it in the A-League. And win by playing that way. I believed we could do it and that what I had in my mind would change the way the club game was viewed in Australia. Before Brisbane I had time to watch and think. Spanish giants Barcelona were playing this unbelievable football. That team had made its mark on football history, that was a legacy. They were keeping the ball for fun, against the best club teams and players on the planet. I thought, *I have to have a piece of that. We have to do that in Australia.*

The approach did polarise people in Australia. Some people were saying it was just keeping possession for the sake of it and couldn't see the benefits, whereas other observers just thought it was amazing. What was different for Australia wasn't different for fans who'd been watching how football was developing globally. I refused to accept that geography should limit the type of football we try to play.

Because these unbelievable players at Barcelona were playing this keep-ball game, the assumption was that you had to be the best in the world to do it. But I took the contrary view, that the roots of that style of game aren't embedded in extreme technical ability. In fact, it taps into the things that are close to Australia as a nation: teamwork, courage, never backing down, never taking a backward step, always being prepared to back yourself and help your mate out. That's what this football is all about. The player in possession always has someone in place to help out. The player in possession has the nerve and bravery to keep the ball under all circumstances because he knows he will have a mate, close by, to help. No one is ever isolated on the pitch. The basic philosophy is togetherness. That wasn't a hard sell. After all, isn't Australian sport's mythology drenched in that sort of stuff?

The start of the process was just drumming into the Brisbane players that this was not about winning and losing. There was some resistance in my first six months, the second half of the season, but by the time we got to the start of the following season there was only one measure for us: the ball. That was all that counted. We were going to keep the ball until it bored the opposition to death, and then we were going to keep it some more. They were going to be so wearied that ultimately they'd just be giving us goals. We were going to obsess about keeping the ball, not giving it away, not even crossing into the penalty area just for the sake of it. Scoring goals wasn't even our main objective, it was keeping the ball. The mantra was unflinching and eventually it permeated all the players. It became a shared obsession.

The first big test of the new playing style came in the fifth game of that second season, against Melbourne Victory. Up to that point we'd drawn two games and won two. The game was away at AAMI Park in Melbourne. The crowd was big and boisterous, the stadium was thumping. There was a lot of expectation around this game. Because I was in my home town with my new team it was a big one for me too. The team and I had generated a lot of news since I'd taken over at Brisbane, and it was very early to be playing the A-League's biggest club on their home turf.

The moment came while Victory were putting us under a lot of pressure, which was to be expected. We had a transition move out of our defence and the ball found its way to Luke DeVere, our young central defender. Luke received the ball and did what he was programmed to do, keep the ball and play it out from the back without reverting to just hoofing it upfield. He coughed up possession and Victory scored. And then, you wouldn't read about it, but five minutes or so later, the same exact thing happened again. Two–nil. You could hear the thoughts of the doubters approach their crescendo: *There's a time to play and there's a time for row Z.* God, how many times have I heard that?

But it was in that moment, when the second 'error' was made, that I knew I had this team. Far from me scrambling to rearrange, redeploy, reset our game plan, I breathed a sigh of relief that the message and its meaning were now embedded. Think about the courage it takes for Luke to try playing out from the back again, the same thing for which he and his team had been 'punished' only moments earlier, and to do it in those surroundings. You make that error the first time and then the ball comes to you the second time, not long after, and your instinct is not to clear the ball, relieving 'pressure', but to keep the ball. I knew at that point the whole thing had crystallised. Call it a turning point, even vindication. These guys believed in what we were doing.

There was no way I was going back after that. This young kid had put his nuts on the line because I'd asked him to, because I'd sold the story of the journey upon which we were embarking. He could have cleared the ball, especially the second time it came to him, and many people would have applauded it. We wouldn't have conceded those goals. But that wasn't our concern. Our aim was higher, our vision longer than this one game at AAMI Park and the three points up for grabs. We lost that game three–nil. The players were probably looking out for a baking in the sheds, because they knew how dirty I get when we lose; I have never just swept losses under the carpet. But when they came back inside it wasn't a case of me tearing strips off the team. I made sure my message was crystal clear: I couldn't believe that those guys had the courage and bravery to do what they'd just done.

From that point they didn't fear losing any more. Their biggest fear became not following the game plan. The ultimate fear of a player is failing through error on a big stage and conceding goals, that feeling that the world is going to swallow them up, well, they lost that fear. Because the world didn't swallow them up. If anything, the coach came in and pumped them up for the manner in which they'd played. We'd lost? Yes, on the scoreboard, on that day. But we played, our shared focus on the ball, and when that message was reinforced fear left the room. That was the victory.

I knew that in time we would eliminate those errors of judgement or execution. But the players now enjoyed the freedom of not being shackled to results. Instead they shackled themselves to our team's philosophy.

It was fun and liberating for them. Keep the ball, move the ball, pass the ball, receive the ball . . . pass, move, keep, pass, move, keep. The adherence to the belief and the play itself was intoxicating. I knew that we'd reached that tipping point and it was going to take a hell of an effort for anyone to stop us from there. As it happened, that was the last time we lost in thirty-six games, an Australian record for club football (in any code).

Brisbane Roar were away. This was going to be a great story, even if at the time many couldn't see it developing or understand what we were doing. Even in the middle of our unbeaten run there was commentary encouraging greater pragmatism. I did find that a bit frustrating because I wanted people to be able to see what we were achieving and how we were doing it. But I guess in their defence, people hadn't been working with us or been privy to our collective commitment, so it might have been difficult to see through the play to realise what the bigger picture was.

To get the model right at Brisbane the first football challenge was mindset. We didn't talk about winning because, truthfully, wanting to win should be an entry-level requirement. I want to win, but winning becomes easier when it's a by-product of something larger, that's my thing. Also, in professional sport, and because of the security of contracts (which is a good thing), players actually lose their competitive edge sometimes. For some players, extra motivation is required to win. Part of their psychology is that their job is to play, but as far as I'm concerned the basis of every professional contract is to win.

The owners at Brisbane had an appetite for change. The club had made the preliminary final two years in a row. They were very unlucky not to have progressed to a grand final. On-field success wasn't far away. It wasn't as though I had picked up the bottom team. Not even close. And I was only there because they'd dropped their previous coach, Frank Farina, owing to a non-football matter. It wasn't because of performance that Frank was sacked. The season hadn't been going that well, however, and there were some struggles. The club felt that it needed something different. They wanted to clear that final hurdle, get to a grand final and win it.

They also wanted a change in the club's culture. Part of that was making the football being played more appealing to the supporters. They had some exciting individuals but there wasn't the collective buzz for the fans. They weren't totally happy with the perception of the club. The yearning for change provided me with the right circumstances to want to get involved. Funnily enough, if the owners had known what the fallout was going to be and how soon after my appointment it would come, they might have looked for another coach.

The mechanics of playing a high possession game were uncomplicated and suited where we were at. Executing this game plan requires players to be in close proximity to each other. Keeping the ball is a numbers game. Can we get more players around the ball than the opposition? If you manage that, passing the football requires an execution over 5 to 10 metres rather than, say, 15 metres or more. People of so-called limited technical ability find it easier to pass and receive the ball over 5 to 10 metres than hitting a 40-metre pass accurately or controlling a long ball like that successfully. Our game at Brisbane was actually about minimising the margin for error, not exposing players to greater risks.

By comparison, in Australia we had always taken the more technically difficult path of hitting long balls and expecting out-numbered players to then do something. Amazing really. The resultant scramble for possession and the fighting for the ball – which apparently was or is a hallmark of Australian play – is an onerous process. It's hard to plan and control the patterns of play when the playing strategy is so chaotic. All this fed into the negative portrayals of Australian football. But I knew getting the Brisbane players into this new short-passing style was nothing more than pivoting on a spot, a change of mindset, whereas others were of the belief that I was trying to turn an ocean liner.

The challenge was to get the players mobile enough to be in proximity. That way, every player knew that when he had the ball he'd have team mates only 5 metres away to help. Enter the Aussie mentality: help out your mate, don't leave him exposed. I knew Aussies would embrace it. Once they saw it and felt it, they'd grow with it. Perhaps a player from another country might have had second thoughts. *I can see what you're doing but I don't care; I'll get lynched if I make a mistake.* It took a bit of work getting the team there, it should be said, but I was confident it would happen. *Even with players breathing down your neck, don't worry – help is close by. Keep the ball. Always. That's how we're going to play. That's how we're going to win.*

We repeatedly faced the attitude of, 'Well, they're doing nothing with this possession.' But for me we were doing something with the ball. Most importantly, while we had the ball we could affect the game. Without it we were no chance. This belief had to seep into the players' minds. As we were building this project, they were the ones exposed to all the commentary. So there was a lot of their 'learning' that had to be reprogrammed.

Players' minds are potentially all over the place. Their motivations and experiences are vastly different.

Cultivating an environment is about reaching critical mass, which is the only thing that can absorb those differences. The strongest thing that binds people together is meaning. There's a point where I'll hear the players using my language, speaking about things in the same way I do, which is a clear sign they're coming on board. They'll communicate with each other on these terms and it reinforces what we're doing. I don't want them reacting to the external, I can't have it. If we kick the ball into row Z when our defence is under pressure then our opponent can't score, obviously. But you know what? Neither can we. My team always has to have that attacking mentality, even when defending.

To play this way we had to be very fit. I thought the general physical output of the league was below what it could have been. Professionalism hadn't really brought a lot of change. I classified the A-League at the time as being the NSL but with training during the day. When he was coach of Sydney FC, Vítězslav Lavička was the first to really have players understand what professional football was, that it wasn't just the difference between training at 6 p.m. or 10 a.m. but something more holistic. In my mind there was no doubt that this big physical gap could be exploited. So at Brisbane we ramped up the intensity in order for the players to produce greater output for longer periods. We pushed their bodies beyond where they'd gone previously. From the moment they woke until they put their heads on the pillow they were footballers, working or recovering, striving to attain the meaning of our journey. We changed how the players prepared, recovered, ate, the whole box and dice. I think this was probably in contrast to other clubs. The A-League became professional with the stroke of a pen, but the evolution to real professionalism was taking more time.

Keeping the ball had virtue. No one in Australia had played in this singular way before and no one really had an idea of how they'd counter it. We repeated the patterns in training and sometimes I'd have to create more vivid pictures to get my point across. I'd show them interchanges they'd completed in the attacking half of the pitch, concise passing moves in very congested areas, and then ask them if they could do it in the front part of the field, what was stopping them doing it in our half, around our penalty area? The answer of course was nothing, other than mindset. It's still a football pitch. The opposition is still the same. It might actually be easier to play out from the back because, typically, defending is less intense from attacking players (or at least it was back then). Every which way we'd cut it, every doubt the players may have brought to this approach was systematically and summarily dispatched. Item by item, improbability by improbability, impossibility by impossibility, hurdles were revealed as navigable, rather than insurmountable. I could see it and as the players began to see it too, the team became irresistible.

This wasn't overreach either. I would never put players in a position where I didn't think they could cope. I would never try to bluff a player into doing something. I'm not a wand-waving spell-caster. What I ask of people might push them, might take them beyond their comfort zone, but it's always short of being reckless with them and their reputations. Sometimes I am perceived to be extreme, but that is more a reflection of a shrunken view by Australians of our football capabilities. In any event, what I was proposing actually played to these preconceptions of what Australian players were about. I wasn't going to expose them to any public derision. I had their back. They came to know that more and more. And from that point there was nothing to fear in the A-League.

The 36-game unbeaten run was something that was growing a life of its own. The recognition was welcomed by me. That was the sort of attention I wanted to bring to the project. Not for selfish reasons but to reinforce what we were doing, and also to put more pressure on the players. To see if they were up to the test, if they'd crack. I believed they would pass the test.

Bizarrely, after the record unbeaten run, we hit a run of losing five games straight. Losing at some point was inevitable. The game that broke the streak was not a pretty game. Against Sydney FC at Kogarah Oval, a venue we hadn't played at before, the wind was howling from the south. They scored one of those accidental and ugly goals, a corner that was slung in and caught by the gale. We couldn't settle into the game and that was that. We lost two–nil. The talk and expectation of the unbeaten run meant that once we'd gotten there, and kept going, there was going to be a letdown somewhere along the way. A lack of focus from some; the breaking of the elastic band as it were. The loss itself shouldn't have been an issue, because we'd not spoken about winning and losing. We let other people have those discussions. I was more worried about the poorer performance in that game, but given the conditions it was always going to be difficult and we just couldn't find a way to win that time.

Then we lost a second game and some people started taking a sideways look at the scoreboard. That's consecutive losses, holy hell! The next game rolled along and the unspoken words were, 'We can't lose this game.' Perhaps at times the actual language changed, maybe even from me. Maybe I started expressing different thoughts. But the whole essence of what we were doing was now becoming a little confused. The next game another goal was conceded and the players started worrying about how they were going to turn things around. In the past, copping a goal was never received with anything other than an automatic response to keep playing our way. Games morphed from exercising our style to becoming must-win because 'the wheels have fallen off'. Some outsiders were delighted that this might be true.

By the fifth loss I kind of checked myself. Whatever was swirling around I stopped and realigned. I made sure my staff were focused and we tweaked a couple of things. We played a back three instead of four defenders, which was nothing major and not a shift in strategy at all, but it got the players focusing on something other than conceding goals and wondering how they could come back. The changes were designed to have players focus on the performance and the process, rather than the outcome.

The best tests for the process are the big games, when the pressure is on. As it was with our first grand final win against the Central Coast Mariners. Down two–nil with four minutes of extra time to go. Where the rest of the watching world is yelling at the players, from the grandstand or at the television, to just get the ball forward, quickly – 'What are you waiting for?' – the Brisbane players are playing their game, keeping the ball, moving methodically, supporting each other. The concepts of time and scoreboard are not relevant factors for them. One goal is pulled back. It's now two–one with a couple of minutes to go. Plenty of Brisbane fans have left the stadium by now. They've given up. Our goalkeeper, Michael Theo, gets the ball in his hands with barely more than a minute to go. Everyone wants him to heave it. The Hail Mary option. But we weren't a Hail Mary team. Michael passes the ball to the player nearest to him, who in turn passes the ball to the nearest supporting team mate, and so on, until the ball has been worked upfield and a corner-kick results. Erik Paartalu scores a brilliant header from the corner. It's two–two and delirium abounds. Only one team was going to win the resultant penalty shoot-out from that point. Brisbane had won their first A-League title and they had done it their way.

One of the things that resonated through the Brisbane success was that the captain can't abandon ship. The battle for the hearts and minds of the players is almost existential. The better the team becomes the bigger the storms are going to be. If you head for the life raft the moment the storm hits, it's highly unlikely you'll be able to get the players back on board once the storm has passed. They'll revert to their own instincts rather than fall back to the plan, and relying on players' instincts and learned habits makes coaching an uncertain thing. Uncertainty is like kryptonite for me. It's not about brave defeat. I want to win and a plan people believe in is the most sure-fire way to win.

Under German coach Holger Osieck, the Australian national team had qualified for its third consecutive FIFA World Cup finals. It was the second qualification through the arduous Asian Football Confederation, our home confederation since we'd moved from Oceania in 2006. World Cup qualification is a significant achievement in itself. Having repeatedly failed to qualify between 1974 and 2006, the Socceroos' mission would become a national obsession, one where big bouts of despair featured heavily.

Not only had Osieck's team qualified for the 2014 World Cup in Brazil, he had also steered the team to the final of the Asian Cup three years earlier, in Qatar. That was a fabulous tournament for Australia. The final against Japan was only lost after extra-time and Australia had plenty of chances to win the match in the regulation ninety minutes. So one could say that the national team was travelling well. Results were positive.

But something was amiss with the Socceroos. There were rumblings. In the meantime I had moved from Brisbane Roar to coach Melbourne Victory. As an onlooker, a supporter, I wasn't happy with what I was seeing from the national team. And then the walls came crashing down for Holger Osieck. In consecutive friendly internationals, first against Brazil and then against France, his team was trounced six–nil. Maybe in another era such defeats would have been accepted, or even expected. But now, in the new era delivered by Frank Lowy's FFA chairmanship, such results made the coach's position untenable. The Brazil World Cup was a matter of months away. The whispers of discontent around the team had become cacophonous. Osieck was dismissed.

Upon my appointment to head coach of the Soccer-oos, I had to transform my observations of the team into a plan – a meaning – to take it forward. This team was supposed to be the embodiment of our national character and I couldn't see that. There was a feeling that we should be subordinate to other nations in football, because we're Australians and we don't know what we're doing. That didn't sit well with me at all.

The foreign coaches who'd come in to manage the national team had rammed that point home. They'd say they loved working with Australians, because their attitude and spirit is unbelievable, they never give up, they always give 100 per cent . . . but the implication was always that Australians were never quite good enough. And they'd organise their teams to play as an expression of that belief. I couldn't stand it. I saw myself being put in that category by them too, as unworthy, and there was no way I was going to accept that. I'll back myself against any coach in the world. Geography doesn't mean that a coach in Germany or Holland or Brazil is better than me. Why would that be the case? I've been fortunate enough to have had a wide experience. I wouldn't cop that. Putting us in a box out of ignorance.

That approach annoyed me because the assessment of our strengths and weaknesses was wrong in the first place, but even then, how can you improve if you don't address your supposed weaknesses. Isn't that what coaches are supposed to do, improve things? Part of what I wanted to do with the Socceroos was to embrace what others thought of as weaknesses and make them integral to our approach.

So when I took over I ensured that the mentality, expectations and language around the team were going to be in direct opposition to everything that had gone before. We weren't going to apologise for being on the field, for taking up space, for being an impediment to other big teams having their way. We weren't going to take a backward step; that was going to be the constant and the players were going to repeat that mantra. I'm speaking literally as well as metaphorically. On the field, the Socceroos were going to be faced with choices. As a defender, do you go into a tackle or do you retreat? We're going in. Receiving the ball, if you have an opportunity to pass forward, do you make that pass or do you play it safe? We're going forward. That is the basis of everything we do now. We take that into every training session, team meeting, friendly game, qualifier or tournament game. Irrespective of the occasion or the opponent, this is what we are about. We will never be a team that meekly believes that our best and only option is to defend in numbers, fighting our way to a commendable draw or hoping that we can catch an opponent on the counterattack. That's not the way Australians like their sport and that was not how Australia's most national of teams, the Socceroos, was going to operate.

I think back to the game against Japan in December 2014, a friendly match in Osaka prior to the Asian Cup. Our world ranking was lower than one hundred. It was all people could talk about, our worst-ever ranking. We hadn't won since the World Cup and, remember, we hadn't won a game there either.

At that time the FFA's Head of National Performance, Luke Casserly, approached me and said Germany, the world champions, had extended an invitation for us to play them in a friendly in March, after the Asian Cup. I was excited by the prospect of testing ourselves against the very best, but I sensed apprehension in Luke's voice. I was waiting for him to say, 'That's great, I'll confirm it with them,' but his response was tempered. He felt obliged to inform me that the hierarchy, which included David Gallop and Frank Lowy, were concerned that given our poor form, if we didn't improve in the Asian Cup, a heavy defeat in Germany might make my position untenable. But all that was going through my mind was what a great test it would be. *World champions versus Asian champions. Wow.*

That's the message I took to the players. I gathered them together after the Japan game and told them that come the end of January team captain Mile Jedinak would be holding up that Asian Cup in victory. Who among them was going to be there with him? It was up to them. I knew where this team was going, for the players it was a matter of who wanted to be a part of it. The players could either be next to Mile on the podium or watching the game on television somewhere. It was going to happen, it was the team we were going to be. That is more than the power of positive thinking, that is belief. Taking the Socceroos job required changing the thinking around the whole operation and changing the perception of what we were and how we were going to do things.

I was confronted with the thinking that I could be radical in the A-League, a competition equalised by things like a salary cap and a limited squad size, but the same couldn't be done on the world stage, against the most proficient players in the world. But I thought that yes we could, of course we could. You can when you've made a decision as a young kid to love something, like football, that is made difficult to love, as it is in Australia. A whole life of that sort of love steels you. If I wanted comfort I would have played Aussie Rules or cricket. There the path to becoming the best in the world is more clearly defined. But my ambitions for the Socceroos were achievable because the disparity in technical quality flattens out when you believe that what you're doing is special. A team may be better equipped but that doesn't mean they've found a greater meaning to what they're doing. When you get to the critical stage in a game, as you inevitably do, having a greater meaning will get you through that moment. Sometimes it will defy every logical thing you see going on around you. *How did he do that, how could this team beat that team? It doesn't make sense.* No, it makes complete sense. It happens when a team that logically shouldn't be in the same stadium as another finds greater meaning in what they are doing. That's powerful.

My approach does put pressure on groups and organisations. It puts pressure on me, too. Pressure gives you focus and it's my drug. People questioning, scrutinising and criticising me. Every word adds more strength because it makes me believe more. When commentary wedges me further towards the periphery, or portrays me as unorthodox, I get stronger and my resolve grows.

It adds to the momentum, because I won't yield to any of those things. They're all part of a dynamic atmosphere. Ideas and criticisms and debate, flying around. It makes me stronger because it brings what I want to do into sharper view, crystallises things around me.

Because when I turn similar questions on myself, in the quietness of my own company, I have to be sure of the answers I find. There's got to be more. There's got to be meaning. I find that meaning on the edge. The trick is taking people with me.

4

WILDERNESS

There are times in life when nothing seems to be happening or going particularly right. More doors are closing than opening. You begin to wonder when, or even if, things are going to change for the better. It would be abnormal in the extreme for anyone to completely avoid those periods that really challenge and shake us. There is a possibility that some people look at my coaching career and think it's all been a bed of roses.

People newer to football's story will sometimes think of my career only as the successful progression from Brisbane Roar championships to Melbourne Victory and then the Socceroos and the Asian Cup triumph. Such a view suggests that the coaching gig is a pretty smooth ride. But whatever success I have had stretches back into the NSL, where I won championships with Hellas as both coach and player. This was a time, though, when there wasn't a lot of recognition for football or its functionaries. The records have virtually been erased. Shamefully, this ignorance has been fed to the game's own administration. Or maybe it's worse; maybe some people dare not speak or acknowledge football's past. Rather than seeing it as an embarrassment, I know the game's history is rich. That it is under-celebrated doesn't change that fact. We should be proud of it. I know I am proud of my small part in it. I don't point this out for reasons of vainglory, we have to embrace the game's history. Football didn't start in this country with the Crawford Report into the governance of Australian football and the establishment of the A-League, so the things that went before should rightly be remembered and celebrated.

But more than all that, focusing on my (relatively) recent success also overlooks the time I spent in the wilderness, with no gig at all. For me it's important to acknowledge the difficult periods too. Life's green shoots can sprout from those tribulations. Positivity must be extracted from the difficult times. While it's little solace at the time, it is a discipline and a duty to take the good from every experience.

When the A-League started I found myself in the coaching wilderness. The feeling of not having a job was made worse by the reality that there were so few jobs going. This was the era with the fewest available professional jobs since 1977 when the NSL began. Given the paucity of openings, an unemployed coach in Australia can face a long time on the sidelines. By the time of the A-League I'd had seven years as coach of the national youth teams, a tenure that ended pretty abruptly. The timing was strange for me. I'd had success at South Melbourne before moving into the national set-up and, after accumulating a lot of knowledge as youth coach, I was sacked at a time when I actually felt more ready to coach elite football than I ever had in my life. I felt I was at the top of the curve. Then the curve collapsed. That pretty much sums up the vagaries of life as a football coach.

It was 2007 and our first venture into the Asian FIFA confederation, after being granted membership in 2006. The qualification for FIFA tournaments would now be through Asia, which would prove infinitely more difficult than Oceania. And as first cabs off the rank, the Under 17s and Under 20s teams I was coaching missed out on qualifying for their world cups. I was shown the door. I still feel it was a knee-jerk reaction, failing to properly understand the cavernous differences between Asia and Oceania. To make qualification more difficult, the youth system hadn't really been swept up with the changes at football's pointy end, where the emphasis was on the A-League and the senior national team. The FFA was in reaction mode and the failure to qualify for those tournaments meant I got the chop. Then, there, no questions asked.

It was surreal, being all set to go with a bundle of knowledge and a world of experience, but nowhere to release all that coaching energy. I had learned a lot of valuable lessons during my seven years traversing the globe with our youth teams. And now there was nothing. Zip. Nada. Worse still, I was, apparently, unemployable. The eight A-League jobs had been filled. I'd just been hauled out of the national teams set-up, so there was obviously no scope for a job there. How had I ended up in this barren landscape?

The possibility of full time employment was looking pretty bleak and it seemed like my reputation was in tatters. As I look back, 2007 is the only blight on my record. I reflect on that seven years as youth coach as being arguably the most enriching experience I had as a coach but, paradoxically, it became the only black mark on my CV.

Naturally, with nothing particular on the horizon, I did occasionally indulge in melancholic questioning of what I was to do from there. But I never seriously wavered from the belief that I would coach again. If a job wouldn't come to me, I would go to one, if needs be. I just had to bide my time and believe it would happen. Meanwhile there remained the need to provide, the pressure of sourcing an income. While I was certain in my own mind about what was to become of my coaching career, eventually, that was not always much of a consolation for the people around me. To them an unemployed but expectant coach doesn't offer much certainty, and certainly doesn't pay the bills.

This was never that much of a worry for me, but it was very unsettling for those around me. And naturally you can't help but sense the unease being caused. I gratefully picked up some work with Fox Sports as an analyst and pundit, which let me keep a hand in the game and kept my profile up. People could hear me talking about issues and realise that I hadn't in fact lost the plot, that there was still substance there. I figured something I said on television might twig with someone down the track and a door might open, they might feel I was worth taking a punt on.

The most difficult part of the journey, however, was that the deep conviction I had that I'd coach again just wasn't matching up with any real opportunities. It was a strange psychological halfway house. Frustration was a constant companion. And I guess the frustration fuelled my analysis of the A-League, on which I was commentating. Knowing I'd eventually coach in the league, the things I'd like to fix via the team I'd be coaching were building up and reaching bursting point. Somehow I'd have to channel that energy away from criticism. I couldn't let the frustration get the better of me and I couldn't let it spill over into my relationships.

I loved the television work but it wasn't really for me. It wasn't as fulfilling as coaching, so it was never going to be a long-term prospect. Even in the emptiest periods it never occurred to me that I might just ditch the coaching and slide into a commentary position for good. I can honestly say it never crossed my mind at the time.

Nevertheless, I was getting very restless. I needed to coach. At first I began conducting sessions with friends' kids in the local park. Helping the parents and the kids develop, have fun and improve. I'd been focused on youth football for the most recent period of my career and this was a small outlet that allowed me to express some of that pent-up energy. I then established a program with Football Federation Victoria called V-Elite. It was quite revolutionary at the time and people still talk about it. I pretty much based it on Clairefontaine, France's national football institute, where I had gone while coaching the national youth teams, to observe their set-up and how they went about things.

These weren't major occupations for me but they kept me active and sane. It also reacquainted me with the realities of part time football; some evening training sessions the group would be full but on other nights the traffic would stop people coming, or homework had to be done, or something like that, and then there would barely be enough players to run a proper session. It was difficult to do what I wanted because I was in the hands of people over whose time I had no real authority. Coaching in that environment is full of challenges. I wasn't advancing my career or making financial progress, but I had to keep going at it anyway, keeping my mind sharp and ready for when the next opportunity presented itself.

That next senior opportunity would be in Greece, in 2008. It came through Con Makris, an Adelaide property developer and businessman who owned a lower-division club in Greece. Con also had football form as a key figure for West Adelaide in the NSL. Like Frank Lowy he develops property, but they have another similarity: both men pulled the team they owned out of the NSL on the eve of, or early into, a new season. Lowy's Sydney City was withdrawn one game into the 1987 NSL season and Makris's West Adelaide on the eve of the 1999 season.

Con remembered me from the NSL days and had probably kept tabs on me since. He had purchased Panachaiki FC, based in Patras, Greece's third largest city, west of Athens. The club was founded in 1891 and, at this time, was in the third division. Makris had gone through a series of coaches before asking me if I was interested in the job. I didn't take much convincing because, if nothing else, it would be work in a full-time program. Being in Greece was a bonus, and the fact that Australian coaches hadn't worked in European club football before also stoked my interest. It wasn't a hard sell to Georgia, my wife, because there was nothing particular to hang around for in Australia. At least it promised to be an experience. I didn't know what to expect, but I had to have a crack.

Coaching Panachaiki was about regaining my confidence. It also provided a practical release for all this accumulated coaching knowledge. It would allow me to experiment with what worked and what didn't, out of the public glare, away from Australia and in a lower league with no pressure. Or so I thought.

I encountered a fantastic bunch of players at Panachaiki. There was a distinctive language barrier because although as a migrant kid Greek was my first language, my proficiency had waned over the years. I didn't realise how much until I got to Panachaiki. It also made me realise what a powerful tool language is and how much my coaching relied on it. I was seriously hamstrung in that initial period. My Greek had to improve. I pestered the board of directors for instructions on how to say something pointedly, with no ambiguity, because in Greek there can be seven ways to say the same thing, each with a subtle difference of meaning. Gradually I grew in confidence. My mastery of Greek improved and, with it, my ability to force the mood and energy of the dressing room.

Aside from the language I also had to read the people, to understand what motivated them as footballers. I was an Australian working in Greece. Although born in that country, to me and to them I was Australian. These were the qualities I brought to the table. But for the players, what does an Australian know about football? How was this guy going to come in and coach them to anything?

Even in this foreign environment and under what would turn out to be intense scrutiny – and keeping in mind that there was nothing else on offer and I had to make this work – I somehow had to establish some unity of purpose for the squad and the club to embrace. I had no walk-up credibility, as I'd had when I took charge at South Melbourne. Even moving into the international sphere with the Australian youth teams, the young players knew about me from Hellas. Here I was totally exposed, out in the cold, fending for myself. I was scratching away at improving my Greek but the players and the training sessions weren't waiting for me to be able to properly link the present continuous or adequately conjugate the past participle.

I found myself in a scramble to gather the things I knew would work, that had worked for me before. Some of the methods that I went on to use successfully at Brisbane and Melbourne were nutted out in Greece. At South Melbourne I had learned not to hesitate to throw youngsters into the team. Equally, I needed to source some experienced players, like I had at South, so that the younger players wouldn't burn out with the added burden.

Over my time I'd found that the earlier promising players are thrown into the mix, the better for everyone. The better players will really thrive and the strugglers will be found out, and no further resources will be used up on them. Panachaiki was going to get that treatment. In Greece I put the young, untested guys into the team en masse and was rewarded for it. I've never been scared to trust kids since. When I went to Brisbane, putting a young Tommy Oar and Luke DeVere in the team was easy. When I went to Victory I had no hesitation in play-ing seventeen-year-old Scott Galloway in the Melbourne derby. One of the young kids at Panachaiki who I made a first-team regular at seventeen, Andreas Samaris, is now playing for the famous Benfica in Portugal and is also a mainstay in the Greek national team.

Coaching Panachaiki was one of the most thrilling experiences I have had because I started from scratch and proved to myself that I was able to remain the type of coach I wanted to be, and still am today, despite the circumstances. I can take my methods and philosophies anywhere and know that they will be relevant and effective. Even where I am unknown or my reputation doesn't carry anything or where there is a communication barrier. If there ever was any self-doubt my time in Greece would have exposed it, but actually Panachaiki washed it away completely. I became a stronger person and coach for the experience. I was convinced that my way worked.

My time in Greece went for three or four months at the back of one season, then through the off- and pre-season, and the first six months of the next season. Spanning those two seasons, my stay was about a year. I remember one of the first games I was in charge of, it was one of those typical Greek league games, very defensive. Here was I, though, trying to bring an Australian mentality of trying to win at every opportunity. I was trying to tell my players not to worry about what was going on around them and what everyone else was doing, that they should just go for it. I quickly realised that my team was just as much part of the problem, though. It didn't take long at all for me to locate where my immediate challenge lay. I always look to see how I can make my team different from the competition and here the answer was obvious.

The game in question was against a local village team and ended in a really, really dull nil-all draw. For the final twenty minutes things descended dramatically. The game became a shambles. The ball was continually being kicked away to waste time, guys were rolling around on the ground slowing things down, arguing with the referee, arguing with each other, pushing, shoving. It was a mess. It's honestly hard to appreciate without having been there how cynical a scene it was – there were two teams playing on a rectangular field with standard markings, sets of fans supporting either team, but that's where it stopped resembling football. At least the way I'd always envisaged the game.

Almost no football was played in that last twenty minutes. As the referee put us out of our misery and ended the match, I brought my guys into the dressing rooms. I didn't rip into them, just tried to tell them that if we were going to be the same as everyone else we weren't going to make any progress. I tried to explain to them that we could be different and that they'd really enjoy the ride. Let's be different. Let's not roll around on the ground. Let's not stop and slow the game down. Let's not engage in pushing and shoving with the opposition. Let's not argue with the referee and his assistants. Let's not verbal and gesticulate towards the opposition bench. Let's get above all that. Let's focus on the ball, that'd be something different. Let's get up and play the game, that would be different. Let's play and let's enjoy this, that would be different.

I was delivering what I thought was – even considering the scratchiness of my Greek at the time – a Churchillian speech. I could see that they were devastated with the game. We'd forged a connection quickly and they knew they'd disappointed me. In full oratorical flight and thinking I had them, I looked over to the back of the room and saw this one guy, a Brazilian, standing with his back to me. He had his head down, standing right in front of the sink. I could hear that the water was running. He was leaning over the basin and it seemed he'd been standing there some time. I wondered what the hell was wrong. Had I really upset him? Was he troubled? Washing his face? Maybe he was crying. Then I heard this whirring sound, I couldn't quite make out what it was. *He can't be happy*, I was thinking. Perhaps I'd gone a bit hard, or used a word that had been misunderstood. He wasn't looking at me so I had to go over and see if he was okay. The atmosphere in the dressing room was taught and subdued. When I got to the Brazilian I found that he was hunched over his coffee machine, grinding beans, oblivious to everything else around him.

I started running questions through my mind about

how a player preparing for a game and for competition can pack in his kitbag, of all things, his coffee machine. It's the first thing you pack after your boots, of course! And then, after a pretty ordinary team performance and being on the end of a collective dressing-down, he then reaches into his bag to get his coffee machine and starts grinding beans. I was amazed. But inside I was also pissing myself with laughter. What a different place and culture, what a different world. I had to bring all these disparate habits and motivations and streamline them into one purpose. It was a bit like herding cats.

The team made progress pretty quickly, though. One memory that will stay with me for some time is hitting the top of the league after a win. There was a team bus that would take us to away games. On this day we'd played about four hours away from Patras and we were on our way back, due to arrive home at about 1.30 a.m. To get back into the city you pass some toll gates and when we were about 5–10 kilometres from them I could see this red glow. I asked the team manager if there was a fire in the city or something. He said, 'Ange, you have no idea what's coming, do you?' I asked him what he meant and he said that the glow was our supporters. They were waiting for us at the toll booths, we were top of the table, they were there to cheer and shout, light flares, honk horns and escort us to the stadium (where our cars were parked).

We arrived at the toll gates. There were probably a thousand people swarming and milling around. They started rocking the bus. There were all manner of pyrotechnics on display. We got off the bus and there were high fives all around, we were being carried and passed overhead on fans' shoulders. It was like a mosh pit, totally out of control. I was trying to keep a lid on things. The players were laughing as they crowd-surfed. I tried to sneak away into the rooms. 'They're calling for you, boss,' came the word. I resisted and just told everyone to relax. It was made clear to me that keeping a lid on this would be a hopeless task. This football team was their life and they were top of the league. It was pandemonium. And we were only ten games into the 34-game season!

Two weeks later we played at home in a game we were expected to win and we drew. I'd packed up my things and was in the office. I was very disappointed and just wanted to get out and find some quiet. The team manager sat me down and said, 'They're out there waiting for us, they're going to kill us, don't go out there.' I asked why, and reminded him that just two weeks prior they were carrying us on their shoulders. He said, 'Trust me, the police have suggested we stay inside.' The manager's phone rang – he told me later – and on the other end of the line was his son who said to him, 'I know you like that Aussie coach but you get out of there without him. They're gonna lynch him.' He laughs telling that story now.

I don't remember those times with fear or intimidation. The cycle in Greek football for players, coaches and fans isn't a weekly one, it's a daily one, rumbling like the sea and just as uncontainable. What I took away from that was the unbridled passion and emotion that the fans invested in their team. The team meant everything to them and I loved that. The whole week the mood of the town would depend on whether the team had won or lost. As the coach I was at the centre of it. I loved every minute. If you win, don't worry about driving anywhere or doing anything, it'll be done for you. Lose and you can't leave your house.

The Panachaiki experience was so enriching. It refuelled my passion and my understanding of what passionate support is. It gave me confidence that my coaching worked. I could engage people, I could collect and steer the energy, I could get results. I now knew that I could deploy those methods irrespective of the environment; whether it be with established players and clubs or starting something completely from scratch.

Returning to Australia I found that I had to bide my time again. The Adelaide United job came up but I missed out. I've since been told that I was across the line but amazingly, just prior to my announcement, it was decided that I was still damaged goods. The club opted for another coach. The circumstances of my departure from the Young Socceroos' set-up still lingered, I was still someone who couldn't be touched. I spoke with Melbourne Heart (now Melbourne City) who were preparing to start their A-League existence, but they wanted to go overseas for a coach and weren't interested in me. Maybe television punditry was my future after all?

Then one night I was doing more Fox Sports television, a game at Etihad Stadium in Melbourne. After the game I came down the lifts and was heading for the broadcast compound to say goodbye to the Fox Sports producers and technicians. As I turned a corner I bumped into Archie Fraser, then head of the A-League. I didn't know Archie and my natural instinct was to not say anything to him. If he came over and said hi, I'd reciprocate. But something inside me just clicked. I was dying to have a crack at the A-League and I thought I should go and introduce myself to him, just in case. I'd never really done that sort of thing before. I'm not a natural networker. I introduced myself and told him of my eagerness to coach. Archie assured me that he knew all about me and that I shouldn't worry. He said they'd been seeking opportunities for me, without my knowledge. North Queensland Fury were a possibility but apparently I'd made some criticism of the club on television so they were off me. Archie made it clear though that the people in charge of the A-League were keeping me in mind.

That was a Friday night. The very next morning, Brisbane Roar coach Frank Farina was done for DUI. I was at my brother-in-law's place when the story came out of Brisbane. Frank had been suspended for the weekend's game so that an investigation could take place. The phone rang, it was Archie Fraser. He said he'd spoken to the Roar's owners and they wanted to meet me on Monday. I wasn't guaranteed the job, only a hearing. Archie was confident they'd be comfortable with me.

If I hadn't reached out to Archie, maybe I wouldn't have been at the front of that queue. I think sometimes you have to state your ambition to those around you. It can be dangerous assuming people know what you want or how you think you can contribute. He might have thought I was happy doing television. From that first phone call from Archie the whole thing snowballed. The Brisbane job was about change and the people there had a real appetite for it, so I knew it would work. Brisbane would be perfect for me.

———

Brisbane was similar to Panachaiki because in some senses I was starting from scratch again. I walked into a dressing room where there were some familiar faces – Matt McKay and Massimo Murdocca I'd coached at youth level – but otherwise the environment was going to be a challenging one. Frank Farina had been a very popular coach and he hadn't been replaced because of results; the players thought they were travelling along quite well. Walking in was tough because I knew I had to win them over. The owners wanted a new way of doing things. I had watched Brisbane pretty closely and knew that a change had to happen in culture and playing style. And in personnel.

I didn't want to target any individual at Brisbane so the first thing I looked to change was the environment in which they were working. That would be the first disruption and would force a reaction. I altered training times; a simple thing really, but some found it really challenging. The way we trained changed too, and the way we talked to each other. Gradually the temperature rose and a lot of conflict resulted.

But I was getting results. Players started coming to me and saying that they wanted out. That was part of the plan, for them to initiate their own departure. I wasn't pushing individuals but the environmental changes were squeezing them. Some didn't like the way I was working, the new standards and rules I was implementing. I had to change the squad and every time a player came to see me I was quite pleased. I didn't lose any player I really wanted to keep.

With the contract and salary cap system, moving players in the A-League environment is very difficult unless the player decides they've had enough. In part it's a game of poker, and the coach can't afford to fold first. I made sure I never gave any indication who was and was not in my plans. I played it evenly. I kept them guessing and kept them all on edge. Some guys read the tea leaves and, to be fair to them, read them pretty accurately. Other players flinched when perhaps there was no need for them to, but I was happy for them to go because it would give me more room to bring people in and change the place.

Others, such as Craig Moore, were prepared to fight it out with me. My view on conflict – and I'm pretty sure I picked this nugget up from Sir Alex Ferguson – is that when you're in a leadership position you don't go looking for conflict, it will seek you out instead. Even on your very best days someone will come to you with a gripe. So if you start picking fights yourself, before you know it you'll be all over the place. I didn't go into Brisbane picking fights. I wasn't going to bawl out anyone just to show that I was in charge, hoping that person would leave as a result.

During this period in Brisbane there was a lot of

conflict coming my way. I had no choice. To use a cricket analogy, I just had to play each one, from the crease and on its merits. Some were easier to dispatch to the boundary than others. Some rose sharply off the pitch and were difficult to handle.

We had one particularly heated team meeting just after we'd lost to Melbourne Victory. Melbourne were too good and there was no problem with us losing per se, but I walked into the dressing room and Charlie Miller, a visa player from Scotland, was cracking gags. Others were laughing too. I know that people handle defeat in different ways, I wasn't going to enforce behaviours for winning and losing. But this set of circumstances presented itself and I had to act. The players' view was that they'd given everything and they should be able to unwind. Their laughing was not indicative of how disappointed they may or may not have been, according to them. But I wasn't happy with that.

So we got to Monday's training session. I told all the coaching and ancillary staff that I wanted them out of the dressing room. It was to be just me and the players. One coach and twenty footballers. I knew what I wanted to do but I didn't know how it was going to go. I had to take on these guys and this attitude. I decided I was going to initiate conflict, to see what sort of reaction I'd get, to see if they cared. And the conversation started nicely enough. I invited comments from the floor. I wanted to hear what the guys were thinking. They said how hard they'd tried, how maybe training could be tweaked a little bit, that sort of thing. They were taking all the rope I was letting out.

Then it started. I turned around and said, 'You know what, I'm looking at a dressing room full of the most unsuccessful players in the seven-year history of the A-League. You know that every other team, bar you and Perth Glory, have played in a grand final? And you're all sitting here smug that you've achieved something because you've made two preliminary finals. I don't see any desire to be better.'

That fired a couple of them up. Charlie Miller piped up and sprayed, 'You can't say that, what have you ever done in the game?' and more to the same effect. There's one cracker gone off, I thought, so I continued, 'You know what is the bigger disappointment? I think there's no leadership in this group. I think the experienced players like having the young guys here so they can tell them what to do but there's no real guidance or leadership, no wanting to make them better.' I looked at Matty McKay, 'After seven years, Matt, nothing, jack shit. And I reckon in another seven years' time, if things don't change, you'll still have won nothing.'

And that was it. Craig Moore just went off his head. Bingo. 'You don't know what you're talking about. You don't have any man-management skills. You're a pathetic communicator. No one in here believes in what you're saying. You've got no idea what you're doing.' And so on. As far as rants go, it was a Champions League effort.

I said, 'That's fine, Moorey. That's your opinion. But you know what, I'm not going anywhere. I'm not going to change so I guess you can either come on board or you can make your decision yourself.' There's no way of sugar-coating things, it was ugly. 'One thing I want you all to understand is that I'm not going anywhere and I'm not going to change. So unless you are prepared to come down this path with me, it's best you make your decisions about your own futures.' That's when Charlie Miller, Liam Reddy and Danny Tiatto all came and saw me. Details were sorted and releases were agreed. Moorey dug his heels in, thinking he'd test this with the board.

We won the next week. We played rubbish but it was one of those games where the players are just so angry that winning is a formality. I saw Moorey afterwards and assured him that I would never attack him personally like that again in front of the group. I saw him as part of the club's future but I needed him to change his mindset. Unless there was a realisation that change was needed from him it was going to be difficult for me to bring the other players along. Understandably, he was a big presence in the dressing room. He just looked at me blankly and I thought then that he'd given up.

The saving grace for me, for us, was that the World Cup in South Africa was only months away so he was still motivated to play. A move came up in the January transfer window which took him to Greece and kept him ticking over until the tournament began. He went to Greece under the assumption that when he came back, I'd be gone. By the time he returned, however, the club had turned around and progress was being made.

The important part of that process was me being absolutely unflinching and strong in my position. Brisbane Roar were embarking on a new journey and I was going to be the person in charge. That foundation had to be laid, right from when I started in October 2009. Even when the board appointed me they'd first said that it would be just to the end of that season, that is, for six months. If things went well they'd extend my tenure. I understood that they wanted to protect themselves because they were still working through a potential termination settlement with their former coach. But I said that they couldn't leave me adrift like that or I'd be dead in the water. With what I was about to do, if the players got a whiff that they only had to outlast me six months, the process would fail. I wouldn't budge. I suggested that they announce a two-and-a-half year deal but that they could get rid of me without any payout. That would enable me to front the players with confidence. And I was prepared to have that clause in the contract, knowing that it wouldn't be necessary. I was happy to give the owners that comfort but they needed to send a signal of solidarity. People needed to believe I was there for the long haul.

The remainder of the season was slow and I would need the coming off-season to put things in place. Some of the younger guys who remained, and had been close to the departed senior players, needed to refocus their energy. They needed to get on board because from that point on no resistance would be tolerated.

Through their application the players went to another level. The whole project just took off from the very first day of pre-season training. I made Matt McKay captain. I was after hungry players, desperate to prove something. Michael Theo returned from a failed UK stint with Norwich City. Kosta Barbarouses wasn't getting a run at Wellington so I swooped on him. North Queensland had shut down so Shane Stefanutto and Matt Smith joined us and were magnificent. Erik Paartalu, a guy who I knew from the Australian youth teams, needed an opportunity. These were all really motivated guys. The influx of new players outnumbered the influential guys already there. Mitch Nichols and Matt McKay would have really isolated themselves if they didn't jump in and, to be fair to them, there was never a hint of regression.

Back when I'd arrived, Matt probably wondered what sort of coach I would be. Perhaps the turmoil was greater for him than the others. He'd known me from the youth teams and, like all those players, probably took away the idea that I was aloof and disconnected. He probably thought I was a bit of a strange cat. When I arrived at Brisbane I imagine that the other players asked him what I was like so he would have told them what his impression of me was. And this mysterious coach, whom the players can't really get a grip on, goes and lobs a hand grenade into the dressing room, exploding the club careers of senior pros. Their existing leader, Craig Moore, just lets rip. Matty must have been joining all these dots together and wondering how it could possibly work. History tells how successfully he has come through the whole thing, including A-League championships, Socceroo representation, stints in overseas leagues, World Cup finals appearances and an Asian Cup winner's medal. He has become a cornerstone for his club, his league and his national team.

To return to Craig Moore, I went on to bring him into the Socceroos set-up later on. It wasn't difficult for me to do that. The bust-up when he left Brisbane

WILDERNESS

wasn't personal at all. And as I said, I actually had it in my mind that he'd remain a Roar player. Craig was a 34-year-old young man then. Players aren't necessarily particularly worldly. Plenty of them have a pretty sheltered life, there isn't always a lot of life understanding there. For some of them it was hard to see what I was doing. I'm prepared to cop that. Maturity sometimes also brings a better understanding of why things happen. So from my perspective there wasn't anything personal in the clash with Craig. The first thing I said to him was that I never meant anything other than to do what I thought was right. His reply to me was sort of the same. He was frustrated and wanted to go to the 2010 World Cup, I was challenging him in a way that he hadn't been challenged before and he didn't like it. At that stage of his career he didn't want to change and so he moved on.

Working with him for the Socceroos was very interesting. I invited his involvement. People may have thought I was offering some sort of olive branch but that wasn't really it. There was a job that needed doing and Moorey was the perfect fit for it. His manner, his speech and his thought processes have changed now. He'd had a fantastic career and had a reservoir of the kind of knowledge and experience that I wanted infused in the Socceroos culture. He'd grown and was now in a perfect place to make a positive contribution.

131

When he returned from the 2010 World Cup he did spend a bit of time sniping at me through the media, but I was prepared to give him the benefit of the doubt. I didn't view his comments as vengeful. The media commentary and scrutiny, it was like water off a duck's back to me. After surviving Greece, which was a real dose of reality, Australian newspaper articles didn't bother me. My time in Panachaiki was the focus of five daily newspapers, three radio stations and two television stations, all covering the team daily. I couldn't breathe without it being news, and if I wasn't doing something worth reporting then the papers would make something up. I remember blowing up about it at first. I tried to ban one journo from the dressing rooms and stop the players from talking to him. I was educated then and there; he had a daily column to fill and my rantings and opposition to him and his style weren't going to alter that fact. If he couldn't get something concrete, he'd make it up. So after that the occasional comment from Craig in the media wasn't going to unsettle me.

It was healthy personal and professional development for me to appreciate that media coverage isn't that important. It isn't something that needs to occupy too much of my thought space, whether it be criticism or praise. When Craig was writing columns, to me it was just part of sport, part of what we do. If it was a reflection of his character I was willing to test that when I spoke with him in person. Part of me likes the fact that people can think you have a mortal enemy with whom you are working side by side. They love thinking there's an adversarial tension in the relationship. I like to keep people guessing, letting them jump to conclusions, speculating.

Ultimately, Moorey performed and was excellent with us at the Socceroos. In Brazil for the World Cup and at the Asian Cup he was outstanding in the role of mentor. And I'd like to think he'll take that experience with him. He calls me now and then and we chew the fat. I didn't set out to have an impact on Craig Moore but if that's happened, all well and good, particularly because you're talking about one of Australia's great players.

5

THE ALCHEMIST'S FIRE

At the start of October 2013 I was head coach of Melbourne Victory. By the end of that month I was head coach of my country's national team. What an incredible six months it had been. Actually, what a ridiculous few years. I hadn't been looking to take over the Socceroos job. I was happily challenged in my role with Victory, working to improve on the first year, where things hadn't finished as I'd wanted, and with a keen drive to push Victory ahead. Anyway, there was no vacancy with the national team, until the incumbent Holger Osieck had overseen consecutive disastrously heavy losses against Brazil and France in friendly internationals. Osieck was sacked and the FFA approached me. It was a job I had to take. Melbourne Victory didn't want me to leave. They spent time haggling with the FFA about my release and while they didn't want to stand in my way, I don't think they were completely happy with how the issue was resolved. It wasn't as though I wanted to leave, either, or had been looking to leave. But as ensconced as I was in the Victory role, I was mindful of my discomfort with where the Socceroos were at. I had to change the course of the national team. The opportunity might only present itself this one time.

At the time a very public discussion was being had about the need to regenerate the Socceroos. Most of the Australian footballing public intuitively felt that the team should have been heading through transition before that point but that the process had never really gotten underway. It seemed that older players had marked their territory and were guarding it closely. Everyone seemed to be crying out for regeneration of the squad, and had been for some time, but there was little experimenting with younger players. The opportunities were very few. The response from those choosing the squads and around the national team organisation was that there were no players pushing for selection. The pool of younger players just wasn't putting pressure on the incumbents, was the line. I just didn't believe it. Of course there would be players worth trying. And I would have thought the role of the coach was to find capable candidates, not just to build his own squad depth and serve his own immediate ends but because one of the duties of the national coach is to expand the talent pool for the sake of the broader game. I was infuriated every time I heard the nonsense that there were no alternatives, and it was something that was being said a lot. I knew it wasn't true. I don't think the public believed it either.

I would take Mat Ryan as one example. As a young goalkeeper, Ryan had made incredible progress and secured a move from Central Coast Mariners to Club Brugge, one of Belgium's most illustrious clubs. Brugge had also been the stopover point for the highly successful careers of Frank Farina and Paul Okon, both of whom played with distinction and achieved plenty in West Flanders. Ryan would be welcome there on that basis alone, and he went on to perform creditably. Ahead of Ryan at national team level was Mark Schwarzer, an undeniable great of Australian football, a hero of the game and a player of immense stature. But Matt Ryan couldn't get a look in, even for friendly internationals. Schwarzer was immovable, even in those games. I questioned that. Matt Ryan was never going to develop without any game time at all. Mark Schwarzer wasn't going to play for ever; he's a legend of the game but he's not immortal.

There was nothing in Mark's form that one could complain about or be concerned with. But I was sensing that players held mortgages on their place in the Socceroos team, which is complete anathema to me. In my world, no one owns a Socceroos shirt. I cannot work where that is the expectation. I would not allow that situation to develop. To achieve what I set out to achieve, people can't get lazy or lose their edge because of a sense of entitlement. I couldn't and wouldn't suggest that Mark Schwarzer was anything other than completely professional and dedicated in his pursuits, one only has to look at his longevity to realise that he has amazing focus. But nobody owns a Socceroos shirt.

I didn't enter the Socceroos fray targeting any particular players. But I made a beeline for the culture of entitlement that I thought had set in and was impeding progress. Only months from the World Cup, there was a dissenting view that transition could wait until after Brazil 2014. The world's biggest sporting event was no place to take untested, primarily young players. The team would get hammered and the players crucified. It would be better, so the argument went, to take it slowly and over the course of the next year, taking in the Asian Cup, blood some prospects further down the road.

Were they kidding? Wait? Go slowly? Don't upset the apple cart? They'd employed the wrong man if that's what was wanted from me. Of course the World Cup is the biggest thing. Of course we don't want to be humiliated. Of course I'd be sticking my neck out, but that's what I do. Not for the sake of it, but to get somewhere special. And as far as I was concerned the Asian Cup wasn't some patsy tournament that could be allowed to come and go, to be used simply to develop some players. Australia was to host this most special competition in January of 2015, only five months after the World Cup in Brazil. There would be no time to blood a new team in between those two tournaments. We had to start now. We had to go to Brazil and find some things out. Then we had to go out and win the Asian Cup. That is what I was about.

I would not wait around to find new playing options after the World Cup. The process would start then and there. No player would be excluded by their age or their reputation, only by form and by how I could rebuild the team and improve its depth. This was going to be a white-knuckle ride through the World Cup and there'd only be limited games to prepare. Plenty of people were nauseated by the prospect. I couldn't control them or their nervous reactions. What I could control was the people in my orbit and channelling their reactions into something positive. Those were the only people I was concerned about. I was putting us out there and I needed them to do the work, but it was going to be me, not them, who'd take the heat. And I couldn't wait for it all to get started.

New in the job, my first real official duty with the team was to attend the draw for the tournament itself. The official draw for the FIFA World Cup is an extravaganza in its own right. A huge event. Glitz, glamour, people everywhere, television cameras, paparazzi, football nobility. I was very mindful of my surroundings and the company in which I'd found myself. I quietly moved in and around as I needed to but tried to keep a low profile. There were plenty of people there purely to be seen, looking to press the flesh. And there was plenty on offer. I was only there for one thing: to see who we'd be playing and to start the planning. I couldn't believe my eyes as our opponents were drawn out of the pots: current world champions Spain, runners-up Holland, and Chile, super-charged by their maniacal coach Jorge Sampaoli. Spain and Holland would need no introduction but it was Chile that caught my attention that day. They were a fabulous team, if not as widely known by the public. Not since the 1990s team of Iván 'Bam Bam' Zamorano and Marcelo Salas had Chile showed such strength. I was really looking forward to that game.

I remember saying to FFA CEO David Gallop, who

was with me for the draw, to sit still and not react to the names of the teams. Cameras would be trained on us and if we so much as mouthed anything (and one can imagine what might have been mouthed when our opponents were revealed) we'd blow our cover. Just sit there and don't react. That was our first play, to look unfazed. I don't know if we achieved that, because I didn't have butterflies bouncing around in my tummy so much as a squadron of Super Hornets.

After the groups were drawn I had to go face the world's media. It was about a 50 metre walk to the press room and I was struggling to come up with the right message. I couldn't say our group was easy – obviously it wasn't – but saying that it would be difficult would set the wrong tone for everything that needed to follow.

While the groups were being drawn my phone had been pinging with messages. On the way to the press room I saw that one of them was from my son, James. As a teenager, and like many at that stage of life, he was usually cynical and monosyllabic. I scrolled through the unopened messages to get to James's. As I opened his text I was expecting something to fit the adolescent profile. Instead I read this: 'Here's your chance to become a legend.'

I'd be lying if I didn't admit to the lump in my throat at that moment. It was a beautiful thing to read, but more so it was gratifying, in a father–son context, to receive something of that substance; the sweeping realisation and reassurance that my son knew exactly what made me tick. That would be my message to the world. That's how Australians respond to a challenge, that's how I look at life, and that's how I'd raised my son. The apple hadn't fallen far from the tree.

This would be the opportunity, thrust upon me with almost no time to prepare and with a squad in comparative turmoil, to realise my vision for the game in Australia and how it was viewed. Indeed, how we viewed ourselves. There would be no shrinking in the face of the challenge. There could only be one approach. I was not going to cower. I was going to expect my team to reset the framework of how our country saw its national football team and its place in the world. That wasn't going to be achieved through damage limitation. Any signals to that effect would be completely inconsistent with my coaching philosophy, my coaching history and what needed to be done with this team. Not for a second would I countenance the negativity about Australian players. If that paradigm was going to change, this was the time to do it. No point putting it off until after the World Cup, or after the Asian Cup. Blow that, we're going to win the Asian Cup. But to do that we had to start finding or making gold right away. To do that you have to get into the fire, and you have to take others with you. Because it's in that furnace of pressure that transmutation will occur and the real gold is revealed. You need to know if you've got the right materials to work with down the track.

Knowing we were playing Chile in the first game, we analysed them a lot. Every game in the last few years, we pored over them. I watched them grow as a team and how Sampaoli had pushed the right buttons with this group. Their form was awesome. In preparing for the World Cup they had beaten England two–nil in England, beaten Germany one–nil in Germany and drawn two–two with Spain in Geneva. That last one was around the same time as Australia getting hammered six–nil by France. Incidentally, Chile led Spain in that game until its death, when Jesús Navas equalised for Spain in the ninetieth minute. These were amazing results.

And the manner in which Chile was playing was instructive. When I looked closer at them I saw Alexis Sánchez and Arturo Vidal had world-class quality. Around them were a team of bulldogs, pulling at Sampaoli's leash and ripping flesh off their opponents (metaphorically speaking). They were an incredible unit. And I thought to myself, *We can replicate what they're doing*. Not on the basis that we too would have five world-class players to call on – we'd be lucky to have two or three seasoned internationals – but that we could become a collective, be really aggressive and get in our opponent's face. Favourites, big teams, don't like it when the minnows take the game to them. If you can hit them the right way you can catch them off guard. They'll expect you to defer to their superiority and sit back, defend in numbers and try to frustrate them. That was what they were used to. That was how the Socceroos had tackled similar challenges under Osieck and his predecessor, Pim Verbeek. I was going to have none of that. My team was going to take on our World Cup opponents with one of the most worn of military tactics, surprise.

To change the whole positioning of the national team, so that subservience would no longer be the modus operandi, we had to be aggressive, even in the World Cup and even when drawn to play the best teams in the world. And physical aggression was only going to be one small part of it. We were going to take the game to Chile, and the others. We weren't going to wait to see what they did and then react. We were going to take the initiative and attack, not sit back and hope to escape without much harm done. Plenty of people back at home would have looked at our preparation and the team we had available and to them avoiding a thrashing would have been an achievement in itself.

My message to the players was that we'd move forward as a team and try to overwhelm Chile in their defensive half of the field. They wouldn't expect it. It would change the accepted order of things. I expected this approach to unsettle our bigger opponents, to give them something to think about. Our first job was to change their approach, to get them thinking. We couldn't do that by meekly occupying the edge of our own penalty area, crowding space and kicking lumps out of any Chilean who came nearby.

With the Socceroos I took a different approach than with Brisbane because possession alone wouldn't faze Spain, Holland or Chile. They would have been used to teams doing that against them, and better teams than us at that. We'd find it hard to unnerve them that way. They could cope with not having the ball because they knew that, with their quality, as soon as they did get it they could do damage with one attack. But I got to wondering what they would do if we went at them straight away, with no hesitation. Not waiting for game circumstances or a desperate late charge, anything like that. If we just lit the fuse, prompted only by the referee's whistle to start the game, and went for them. That when we lost the ball we'd immediately tear after it and move forward, again and again, relentlessly. I thought that would be something very different for them in dealing with the likes of us. That would be our element of surprise.

It's crazy that we only had three or four games before the World Cup to start imprinting that in the minds of the players. That was a real challenge. Given the shortness of time and the injury toll to key individuals before the tournament (we'd lost Robbie Kruse, Rhys Williams, Tom Rogic, Josh Kennedy and Trent Sainsbury) I wasn't even really sure who the best eleven players were going to be. The best-case scenario was that we were going to be very thin in some departments. But I couldn't abandon what I knew needed to be done. In fact, the more depleted the squad, the more we had to push on. Caution would have betrayed everything I stood for and everything I'd communicated to the players and staff. Of course the risk was high, but the potential returns were even greater.

I needed to instil the belief in the team that at every opportunity we were going forward, on the field, off the field, in the minds of the Australian public and in the eyes of the watching world. Early on in my tenure that message was clear, although the details of what that was going to look like weren't. I had it in my mind that we'd model the approach on Chile because it was relevant, but I didn't verbalise that to the group because I didn't want them subsumed with thoughts that they were a replica of another team. Anyway, it might have daunted some of the younger guys, being compared to players that in all likelihood they were in awe of.

I didn't want them any distance down the track, in their own minds, before we'd even taken a first step.

But in that first game at the Arena Pantanal in Cuiabá everything got swept aside in a furious opening quarter of an hour. We went down two–nil and everything could have turned to shit. It was looking likely. Emotions were swirling and the atmosphere was searing. Chile was on fire and we were looking like we might come apart at the seams. We'd spoken about doing the opposite of what they'd expected of us. Attacking them using their own game. Being aggressive with the ball, as well as without it. We had worked on playing through their intense and energetic press, to turn them around and have them start questioning themselves. Everything they were going to do to rattle us, we'd turn back on them. Even with that drummed into the players, it's another thing altogether to be on the field, with a very inexperienced team, being terrorised by the power, skill and movement of such an opponent.

And it could have turned nasty. At two–nil down many people are thinking, *Oh no*. There were a lot of Australians who'd travelled to Brazil and their World Cup was seemingly over ten minutes into the tournament. This wasn't how it was supposed to be. The World Cup in Germany in 2006 seemed eons ago. And four years earlier, in Durban, Germany had effectively squashed our tournament hopes with a four–nil drubbing of the Socceroos in their opening game. In Cuiabá we were heading for the same abyss.

But the fans and other observers only have a view of what happens on game day. They're not privy to the preparation. To the construction and communication of messages and meaning. They have no real insight into the mental state or attitude or readiness of the players, or their confidence levels. I'd only been in charge for a few games and none of them had yielded any particularly encouraging results. Most fans only knew of me through what I'd done at the Roar and Victory, and the A-League was a long way from where we found ourselves against Chile. Prior to the World Cup we'd had a blistering opening in a friendly against Ecuador in London, leading three–nil after half an hour. But that lead eroded and we eventually lost the match four–three when, late in the game, Alex Wilkinson coughed up an error. That was Wilko's Socceroos debut. Here he was again, in the opening match of a World Cup, in an inexperienced central-defensive partnership with Matthew Spiranovic, trying to sandbag against a rampant Chile team. Our own fans were expecting the worst. They had no idea as to how the team was placed and what a reservoir of strength was available. To them it was all looking terribly fraught. And the Chile fans were giving them plenty.

When we went down by two goals, I'm sure Chile expected us to shrink and try to save face. That they could hit cruise control. But what they saw was us coming and coming and coming. I was witnessing another moment as I had with Luke DeVere at Brisbane. I have to say I was surprised by the players' response, the voracity of their belief, because the pressure was intense. I couldn't say, hand on heart, that at two–nil down I wasn't worried. That would be disingenuous. I wondered if I'd asked too much of this group. This was a new team against a terrorising opponent. Goalkeeper Matt Ryan was young and only in his fifth game. Ivan Franjic was trying to stop Alexis Sánchez. On the other defending flank was Jason Davidson, only just making his way and now trying to stem the tide of Chile's left side where Eugenio Mena and Eduardo Vargas were running amok. In midfield Jorge Valdívia and Vidal were on fire. Alex Wilkinson wouldn't have been in the national team under any other coach and here he was pinned to the canvas, struggling for oxygen. Matt Leckie was just getting his career going in Germany. We had Mile Jedinak and Timmy Cahill and Mark Bresciano, that's about it as far as experience was concerned. Deep in the fire, I did wonder if I'd asked too much.

Amid the mayhem, a moment crystallised; I was fully prepared to wear whatever would come of this.

I may have asked too much of the players, but this was exactly what we needed to find out. If it collapsed, the players would be safe and I'd be crucified. I was prepared for that. There was quite a queue forming anyway. I'll remember that crystallising moment forever. I couldn't know how much would blow back my way but however much it was, I'd cop it and we'd move on. Or not. I might have been let go by the FFA, but I wasn't going to be intimidated by that possibility.

A quarter of an hour into the 2014 World Cup we were seeing exactly what this exercise was intended for. To see where we were at and make a statement about where we were heading, to see how far short of that mark we were and what we needed to do to improve. Playing against the best in the world will teach you that. There was no way I was going to sacrifice that opportunity for the sake of damage limitation or to save my own arse. There was no way I was going to shout from the sideline that the plan had changed. Imagine what that would have done to the team.

I'd well and truly passed that point already by not selecting skipper Lucas Neill for the tournament. And as other guys retired, such as Mark Schwarzer and Brett Holman, the inquisition would be ongoing. I wasn't going to hide behind so-called experienced players or the idea that we needed some older heads to steer us through. I'd gone beyond that point with the players, with the staff, with the media, and it would have been duplicitous of me to fall back to that approach. I wasn't even vaguely interested in it anyway.

At two-nil down I was thinking, *There's nothing I can do about it now.* I couldn't run out onto the field and do something. I couldn't even shout any instructions, in that steamy arena the din was so skin-pressingly loud I couldn't even hear myself. It was the players who were out there and they were the ones exposed. All I could do was see how they were going to react. There's a part of me that must have known that no team of mine would ever chuck the towel in. I don't prepare teams that way. No team of mine is ever going to go out there, even in the worst possible cir-cumstances, and not believe in what I've said to them. So I couldn't have gotten it that wrong. I didn't believe I'd gotten it that wrong.

The way they performed – and I saw it well before half time – the reaction came and we grew into the game. The players stemmed the tide. It was an amazing, affirm-ing thing. I knew then that I hadn't gotten it wrong. Maybe the players were oblivious to what was in front of them. Maybe their inexperience and naivety protected them a bit. It looked for a while as though we could get done by six or seven, and perhaps more experienced players would inadvertently have brought something like that on. But the youngsters were just so determined to do what I had been telling them. It was an irresistible force. There was no room in their minds for them to start deviating from the plan, to think of consequences.

We began to create a couple of half chances. Then Timmy scored. The belief that went through the team was palpable. Potential disaster had been averted by commitment to the core of the plan and dogged determination to see it through. The goal brought everything to life. The team was away. Just before half time I saw the Chile leaders, Vidal and Sánchez, in heated exchange. I remember Timmy and Mile looking at me and even in the raucous noise it was clear what they were saying: 'We've got them.' They both sparked up and a ripple went through the team. That was important, as the two most experienced players they were probably also the most worried.

The second half was another improvement and we created some great chances. We didn't win the game but the battle had been won. The rag-tag Socceroos, depleted, inexperienced and in transition had risen to a very significant challenge and on the biggest stage there is. Chile was a gun side and we'd handled them.

That's what I wanted out of the exercise and I felt strongly that we could push on now. There was really an amazing outpouring that day, an understanding of

My dad with his brother and niece in the early sixties. Family and culture were important foundations but, in the end, economic realities meant it was a life he had to leave behind.

My dad not long after he arrived in the country, beer in hand and trying to fit in to the new culture. The early days were tough but friends made through football helped ease the path.

That's me on the right, posing for the camera, somewhat out of character.

The Prahran High School football team, 1978. I'm in the front row, fourth from the left. We're wearing the hand-me-downs from the previous year's footy team – sleeveless tops, tight shorts.

Best and fairest in the South
Melbourne Under 16s.

Enjoying a drink with Dad.

The football family at South Melbourne. I'm second from the left, bottom row.

As coach of South Melbourne. I'm in the middle, in the tracksuit, and Paul Trimboli is immediately to the left of me. TONY FEDER/ALLSPORT

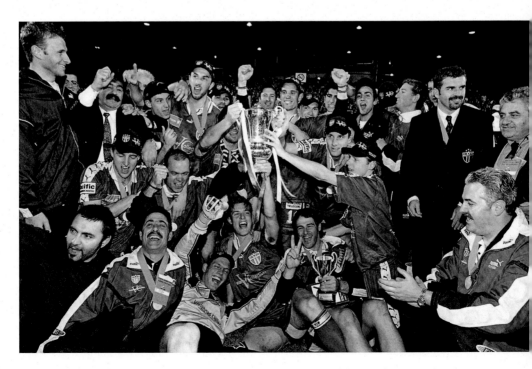

Celebrating back-to-back NSL grand final victories with South Melbourne in 1999.
STUART MILLIGAN/ALLSPORT

Mark Viduka, Craig Moore, Tim Cahill and Harry Kewell at the 2006 World Cup,
a high-water mark for Australian football. We no longer have the same youth development
infrastructure that helped produce some of the players of that golden generation.
SANDRA BEHNE/BONGARTS/GETTY IMAGES

Losing my job as coach of the national youth teams in 2007 was a low,
but the seven years I spent in that role were arguably the most enriching experience
I've had as a coach. MARK DADSWELL/GETTY IMAGES

Early in my first full season with Brisbane we lost three–nil to Victory. Luke DeVere was twice caught out trying to keep possession at the back. But it was in this moment, as Ricardinho stole in to score the second, that I knew my message had become embedded in the Brisbane team. MARK DADSWELL/GETTY IMAGES

In 2012 Brisbane Roar won their second grand final in a row. What made me proudest was that we had proved the naysayers wrong. We'd won it our way, with a style of football the A-League hadn't seen before. BRADLEY KANARIS/GETTY IMAGES

Del Piero had a huge impact on A-League attendance and viewership. We'll have to wait to see what long-term difference his presence made, but signing international marquees alone won't be enough to grow the domestic league. DANIEL KALISZ/GETTY IMAGES

Besart Berisha and Thomas Broich are two of the best players in the A-League, but we've sold ourselves short by not marketing players of their quality the same way we do 'big name' international marquees. These two shouldn't be able to walk down the street without being recognised. SCOTT BARBOUR/GETTY IMAGES (LEFT), BRADLEY KANARIS/GETTY IMAGES (RIGHT)

With FFA CEO David Gallop and FFA Chairman Frank Lowy, announcing my appointment as Socceroos head coach in October 2013. MATT KING/GETTY IMAGES

Craig Moore and I didn't see eye to eye when he was a player at Brisbane Roar, but I brought him into the Socceroos set-up going into the 2014 World Cup. His knowledge and experience were something I wanted infused in the squad. CAMERON SPENCER/GETTY IMAGES

Training in Sydney in November 2013. For the players the World Cup would be all about confidence. I'd take on the burden of any negative consequences – for them Brazil had to be about building belief, not getting results. MATT KING/GETTY IMAGES

With Lucas Neill after what would prove to be his last match, against Costa Rica in Sydney, November 2013. It was the right decision to drop him from the team, but I was dissatisfied with how it played out. MARK NOLAN/GETTY IMAGES

Matt McKay, born and raised in the NSL and the A-League, knows exactly what Australian football is all about. In Brazil he stood toe-to-toe with Spain's midfielders, the best in a generation, and came out with great credit. JEFF GROSS/GETTY IMAGES

I don't measure myself by other people's expectations. I don't care what platitudes big-time opposing coaches have for me. After our World Cup game Louis van Gaal wouldn't shake my hand – I liked that, it told me we were on the right path.

ALEX GRIMM – FIFA/FIFA VIA GETTY IMAGES

Giving a press conference to begin the hundred-day countdown to the 2015 Asian Cup, but the team's sights had been set on winning this tournament since before the World Cup.
RYAN PIERSE/GETTY IMAGES

Overseeing the final training session before the start of the Asian Cup. We had an opportunity to write a beautiful new chapter in Australian football history and I was drilling that into the players from the beginning. WILLIAM WEST/AFP/GETTY IMAGES

The Asian Cup final against South Korea, Sydney, January 2015.
STEVE CHRISTO/CORBIS VIA GETTY IMAGES

Winning the Asian Cup on home soil. Tim Cahill was immense, the support from
the stands unbelievable. It was the culmination of a journey that had begun a long
time ago, the result of the belief and the narrative the players had internalised.
We'd set our eyes on this summit and we reached it. MARK KOLBE/GETTY IMAGES (TOP LEFT),
BRENDON THORNE/GETTY IMAGES (TOP RIGHT AND BOTTOM)

Massimo Luongo was voted player of the tournament at the 2015 Asian Cup and then longlisted for the Ballon d'Or. That's exactly the sort of thing we should be celebrating, instead some were embarrassed by it. RYAN PIERSE/GETTY IMAGES

With captain Mile Jedinak during the friendly against England in May 2016, preparing for the World Cup 2018 qualifiers. MARK RUNNACLES/GETTY IMAGES

With Andreas Samaris, after a friendly against Greece in Melbourne, June 2016. Andreas became a first-team regular at seventeen while I was coaching Panachaiki in Greece.

what could be achieved. Nobody expected anything of us. I knew what I was aiming for but couldn't be sure of what the players, deep down, thought or felt. The performance spoke volumes to me though. We spoke a lot about expecting plenty of ourselves. It was a belief based not on history but on what we wanted to become, what we wanted Australian football to become. Post-match the dressing room was drained. The players had given everything and we'd come up just short on the scoreboard. We should have gotten something out of that game. At two–one down we had some great chances and could, maybe should, have scored. Chile's third goal came deep in injury time and made the scoreboard unduly lopsided. The team was tired but sparked by the strength of the performance. Then the news came through that Holland had beaten Spain five–one . . . and we had to play them next.

'Your chance to become a legend.'

The team met and I said to the players that after the Holland game everyone was going to be talking about us, the team that beat the team that had beaten the world champions. This game was my special target. No one in the world was going to expect what we were about to deliver, and we were going to beat this Dutch team. I believed it in my bones.

All the messages coming in were daunting. My assistant coach, Ante Milicic, was telling me how awesome

Holland were, ripping Spain – *Spain* – to pieces. Arjen Robben, Robin van Persie, they were on fire. But I was convinced this was our game. Holland would play three at the back believing they'd dominate us, but we'd let Matt Leckie loose on them, they'd have to worry about his speed and power. Could *they* handle *him*? We'd get at them. Holland wouldn't be happy playing out from the back and we'd get Timmy to close down their goalkeeper because he wasn't good with his feet. They weren't going to expect us to go at them because we'd lost to Chile and they'd beaten Spain convincingly. They were going to think we'd be planning on saving face. I wouldn't let up though, I felt we were going to cause an upset.

Well, if the players thought I was crazy, they didn't show it. They believed me. Because they wanted to believe the message too, and that's important. So used to being told what they're not good at, by a series of coaches, they were buzzing that the plan was based on what they were capable of and should try to do. It was all positive. It wasn't bravado on my part, putting this plan to them. This was the Prahran High School coach living out his football dreams. What the hell was I doing coaching at a World Cup? But I'll always keep going, making people believe things can be achieved, until someone blows full time and tells me it's time to go. Until then, it's full steam ahead.

The strength I've derived from that coaching fantasy is beyond description. And when life is breathed into those dreams by a group, by coaches and players who've bought into the story, it's enervating. It's a truly incredible, almost an out-of-body experience. Then I'd ask myself, well, why wouldn't I be here? I'd always imagined the likes of Holland coach Louis van Gaal in a game against me, pulling his hair out and abusing the referees, the officials and his players. And an Australian team being the ones doing it to him.

So I fed the fantasy. I was supposed to be there. It was no accident. I had earned this place in time and we were Australians. We weren't going to shy away from it and not give our very best. We were sticking to what we'd set out with rather than carrying a weight put upon us by outsiders who didn't believe we were capable of much. I wasn't a foreign journeyman career coach who'd jetted in for a World Cup jaunt with a country that doesn't know any better. I had skin in this game and its future. I believed in what we could do, and there was no better place for it than a World Cup.

I know I can't be the only Australian capable of this. My upbringing was not unique. I'm not confined by my geography and neither are others. Circumstances have moulded other capable people. I wonder if the leaders of our game comprehend this, that it can be done, in an Australian way, by an Australian coach and by

Australian players. When they watch Matty McKay, born and bred in the Australian game, in the NSL and the A-League, keeping the ball against Andrés Iniesta and Spain – are they seeing how significant that is? How poignant? I fear many of them are still beholden to other, diminished views of Australian football. Too often their only reference point is how hard this business is to run, which they think must result from the fact that we're no good at this game. People have been saying it for a long time so they think it must be true. Commentary like that is way off the mark. Even without winning a game at the World Cup in Brazil, I hope we went some way to changing that thinking. All I am asking people to do is open their eyes, see what's before them, and appreciate the context.

Hopefully the World Cup challenged the thought that Australia isn't capable of going beyond a pre-ordained station. We can at the World Cup and we can domestically with the A-League. There is no reason to restrict football and deny its opportunity to grow. The negative stereotypes are perpetuated by people who either have no idea or are serving a vested interest; neither viewpoint should get anywhere near running Australian football. If people at that level aren't excited about the game's potential and taking the necessary risks to realise it they should move aside and let someone in with the requisite, unbridled belief.

I remember being at a corporate function for FFA sponsors after the World Cup. It was a kind of workshop day and Matty McKay was invited along, there as a bit of window dressing. I don't know what people thought of him or if they even knew who he was. There was one session where he was being interviewed about his experiences in Brazil. Matty McKay, born and raised in Brisbane, is a product of the Australian system and spawned from the Australian football culture. Here was a guy who had taken on the best midfield of a generation – Spain's Xavi, Andrés Iniesta, Xabi Alonso, Cesc Fàbregas, Juan Mata, David Silva – playing them at their own game and holding his ground. If it had been Darren Lockyer or someone else like him in the chair, plenty of the attendees would have been fawning over his exploits against NSW in State of Origin. But Matty McKay had taken on the very best the entire planet had to offer and come through the experience with credit, and it probably barely registered with people. His achievement alone, in that game against Spain, was stunning. It is incumbent on the game's leadership to ensure that is recognised. Sometimes I wonder if they even get it.

The beautiful thing I remember about that corporate event was the look on Matt's face, which revealed a delightful duality. Part of him was actually thankful that someone had noticed the magnitude of what he'd done. The other part was a mixed and confused sense of, *Did I really do that?* Sitting in the audience I sensed some people also wondering how this could be. Matt McKay plays for Brisbane Roar, not Barcelona; he couldn't have done that. The truth is not everyone can play for Barcelona, but that doesn't mean they aren't capable players. The prevailing attitude is that Australians are sub-par. The point of the World Cup in Brazil was to show ourselves and anyone else who'd cared to look that that wasn't true, that Australians could mix it with the best in the world.

On that score, I'd say mission accomplished.

6

THE POWER GAME

I might have realised that as Socceroos coach I was entering a different world. The world of mega-power and big business. Not because of the job itself but because Frank Lowy, the founder of Westfield and a former director of the Reserve Bank of Australia, had assumed leadership of Australian football. That is the world in which football, by association, now found itself. Being Socceroos coach meant I was automatically walking into something I'd never really seen. I guess the big question for some was how that would affect me. Only time would tell how the relationship would play out, if I would remain true to the things that had delivered me there in the first place.

I arrived at the Westfield office in Sydney, the headquarters of the world's largest retail property development operation, for my first meeting as Socceroos coach with (now former) FFA chairman Frank Lowy. I walked into reception expecting to find the elevator and head straight up to see the chairman. Folly, of course. I was met by a security guard who checked my identity. 'Ange Postecoglou, from the FFA,' I reported, and was received warmly before being escorted inside the citadel. I found myself alone in a lift before the carriage halted and I was greeted by more security. I finally found my way to the chairman's office. The place was sparkling. Beautifully styled and maintained but not ostentatious at all. It sort of felt like *Alice in Wonderland*, falling through the rabbit hole into another world, eyes wide open and mouth agape.

The chairman greeted me with a big hug and smile. 'Hello Angie.' He's the only person who calls me Angie, except maybe long-time football journalist John Economos and my mum. The contract negotiations had all been completed and the formalities executed. This was the first meeting of my era, as it were. Lowy began.

'Sit down, sit down,' was the invitation. 'I've always wanted an Australian coach for our team. I wasn't sure if it was the right time but you're the right man so now is the right time. You speak so well and you're great for the game and you're a very good coach.' He kept pumping me up and pumping me up. I felt like I was about to take off. Then he said, 'I had this vision. I remember once, this Czechoslovakian coach. He had grey hair. I asked how long he'd been in the job and they told me fifteen years. Angie, I want your hair to turn grey in this job.'

The pump-up continued. I was airborne now, soaring; I felt like I was looking down on the skyscraper I was in. I thanked the chairman and reaffirmed the fact that I was honoured to be in the position. I assured him I wouldn't let him down and that I knew I could do a good job for him, for the game. As I was talking I got the real sense that his focus had been diverted, that he wasn't really listening. Words were coming out of my mouth but Lowy's mind had gone somewhere else. I started thanking him for his time and preparing to leave.

He re-entered the atmosphere and said, 'I just want to tell you one more thing. I love to win.'

The room instantly became clammy.

'I love to win' just hung in the air. The sentimentality of the pump-up fell away. It was unspoken but very clear; regardless of the nice feelings, ultimately the only measure would be winning. Lowy wouldn't tolerate losing and I wasn't to think the conviviality of the meeting superseded that. The picture was made very clear to me.

CHANGING THE GAME

I wasn't fazed, although that special *Alice in Wonderland* moment ended pretty abruptly. I was completely okay with the sentiment and wouldn't have wanted things any other way. I understood who the chairman was, how he'd gotten that job and how he had been so successful in business. In that one exchange he showed how he could draw me in and make me feel good while also putting what was required from me in no uncertain terms.

I remembered, almost in the moment, a yarn spun by the commercial boss at Melbourne Victory, Jimmy Christou. Victory had invited Frank Lowy to one of their very successful Victory in Business corporate lunches. Lowy was sitting at his table having his lunch and, Jimmy as he always does, grabbed a club sponsor to introduce him to the guest of honour, in this case obviously the FFA chairman. Christou brought over the boss of one of Victory's major sponsors at the time. Together they approached Lowy's table and Christou tapped the chairman on the shoulder, making the introduction. 'This is our major sponsor, blah, blah, blah.' The chairman stood up as Christou continued.

'That's good. Do you run a good business?' asked Lowy.

'Yes,' came the proud reply, chest out and shoulders back. 'We're the third-biggest supplier in the industry. We're really successful. This is the first year we've had

162

a twenty per cent market share.'

Frank looked at him and said, 'That's fantastic. Now you go and work on the other eighty per cent and I'll have my lunch.'

Jimmy Christou's face deflated faster than a punctured balloon. The sponsor got a lesson in what Frank was about.

I should hasten to add that the exchange was personable and not cruel. But it was a reflection of the ruthlessness and clarity embedded in the Westfield success story, and I very much respond to that sort of thing. I reckon if I'd spoken with Lowy about his vision for Westfield it would have been strikingly clear. There would be no 'depends' in his language. 'Failure is not an option' was his catchcry in the early days of the A-League and Australian football's reconstruction. It probably is still the central tenet of the faith. That doesn't daunt me, it appeals to me. I always feel people like that are going to respond to my way of doing things in football because they operate the same way in their own world.

It's very important for me to appreciate the particular world inhabited by my employers. Materially, their world is usually very different from mine. I'll eagerly learn from them, respect them, try to understand more and more about them, but I won't speak to their world. They've been successful for very specific and very good reasons. And the reverse is true too. Football is my world and there I am the boss. My success in football is also achieved in a very specific way. There are parallel principles, certainly, but the details of the mechanics are very different. I keenly observe the methods of those around, but I'm also mindful of bringing key people on board with how I operate on the football side of things, especially where their interests are directly impacted.

My early experience at Brisbane Roar is a good example. There was a very personable ownership group at the club, who'd derived success in their various business ventures. They were great sharers of their experience. When I took over as Brisbane coach, some radical things needed to take place. Well, they weren't that radical from my vantage point, but there was the real chance that others might have a different view. The owners and major sponsors, Coffee Club and Luxury Paints, needed to be brought along on the journey of change, not merely have it thrust upon them. I had to keep them abreast of what was happening. They didn't want any surprises and I didn't want to surprise them. Surprise environments are incongruous with control environments and, as far as I can manage, I work to be in control of things. That's my nature, to exert control. Keeping players on edge about my thoughts is not about waiting for the moment to surprise them. On the contrary, I make the coaching and playing environment very consistent, the rules and behaviours and patterns never change to any great degree. Surprises just spook people. Owners and employers don't need to be spooked.

I couldn't let the Roar owners discover things second-, third- or fourth-hand. Everything had to come directly from me. They needed to be close to the process and they needed to find some comfort in what was about to take place in the football operation of the club. I was going to pull Brisbane Roar apart and then rebuild it, and it was the owners who needed to give me the space to do that work. It wasn't going to be a completely comfortable experience but that's what they'd employed me for. There is a difference between agreeing to the task ahead and the feeling when the wrecking ball goes through. I still needed the ownership to be included in the narrative, I couldn't leave them as spectators. The reality was also that I hadn't coached in the A-League before, so they were taking a risk on me to begin with.

As part of the shake up, some big name players were going to head out the door. 'But Ange, Charlie Miller was voted best foreign player in the league last year, how are we going to replace him? Liam Reddy is the best goalkeeper and Craig Moore is a massive personality.' If I'd just told them not to worry, that I had everything under control and they should just let me get on with my job, they might have wavered. Having the club's leadership close to the process and informed about what was happening, and what needed to happen, meant that they were endorsing the new direction. That didn't mean I would be any less in charge of that direction.

I needed their seal of approval, and that meant not only sharing the dismantling of the team but also the way I was going to rebuild it. I told them I'd found this player in Germany, he was unbelievable. I was going to ask them to pay more for this player than anyone at the club had previously been paid within the salary cap (that is, a non-marquee player). I could have just demanded his recruitment but I needed them to invest in the process. They'd been through a very tough six months. Their new coach was mowing through the squad, as I'd said I would, and they probably got a bit squeamish when they saw what that actually meant. The team was taking on a new look. They couldn't know if it was going to work. They were putting more faith in me than they first thought they might. I'd kept steaming ahead. I made sure I took them with me. I wanted them to be excited, not frightened, by what we were doing.

So we sat in my office; Emmanuel Kokoris, Claude and Serge Baradel, Emmanuel Drivas, all football lovers who'd put their financial nuts on the block for the Roar. We got comfortable in our seats and I turned on the projector and I showed them highlights of Thomas Broich. Their jaws hit the floor. What a player. I told them about driving across Europe to get to Thomas, having coffee with him. I told them how much money he was being paid and that he had been groomed for years to be the next big thing in Germany. By the time I'd said that he was going to cost $300 000 they'd already collapsed into a lather of 'we must get this bloke'. That was crucial. When Thomas proved to be such a success, it meant the people who'd made it possible felt deeply part of that success. They could rightly claim that they were part of the recruitment process. Thomas was a massive investment. They could have taken the view that the club was reeling from the renovation work and gone down an easier path. Hopefully, however, they've all enjoyed the beautiful new house that was built as a result. They should rightly be proud of their work.

As the Socceroos were going to go through a similar, perhaps more painful transition, I would also have to sit down with Frank Lowy and explain the same sorts of things to him. I had to put the young kids into the team and I had to do it immediately. We had to find out who was good enough and who wasn't. He had to be included in that story and his nerves, if there were any, needed to be eased. I believed there was some exciting talent but that it hadn't been exposed to competition yet, or given any sort of chance. I had to make that very clear, although Lowy was already aware of what was likely to be in store. He had to understand that, while it mightn't be obvious in the short term, by the end of the Asian Cup the course would be very clear, and that it would be a successful journey. 'I don't like to lose' rang in my ears. There would be storms ahead, but the chairman had bought into me and in doing so he had bought into the process. That's what he'd hired me for and that's what he was going to get. To get anything worthwhile done at the end of it would probably require plenty of discomfort along the way.

I had to keep telling the story of the inevitable emergence of players like Massimo Luongo, Trent Sainsbury; that guys like this would be making Australia very proud. The fact that no one knew who they were when my Socceroos tenure started was irrelevant. If someone had taken a punt on players like that a bit earlier there mightn't have been the need to get me in when they did. These players' ability and potential had nothing to do with their obscurity or anonymity. Their potential just needed unlocking. I knew they possessed the talent.

The conversations were endless and the energy

expended in reinforcing the message was exhausting. Matt Ryan was going to be a world-class international keeper, he just needed games. Tom Rogic the same. I believed everything I was saying. I didn't extend platitudes to get the job or to appease the chairman. Sometimes coaches, or people in the corporate world, get intimidated by the status of their employers and revert to telling them what they think they want to hear. They are afraid to include them in the journey in case something goes wrong and it comes back to bite them. Having that sort of frailty isn't a recipe for success, particularly when you're working with successful people. They can sense weakness and insecurity a mile off. They might ask some tough questions but in the end, in my experience, they'll respect focus and determination more than someone who flutters with the wind. It just makes winning the battles along the way – finance, budgets, players, media, opposition, criticism – so much easier to handle if you've held a strong, honest line while including people, even powerful people, on the journey.

The super rich, the super powerful, the super connected, they all get the same approach from me. Because when I talk football, those people are coming into my world. I'm not talking about shopping centres, I'm not talking about coffee shop franchises or mining leases – I wouldn't be so presumptuous. I'm talking about my world, the world I've imagined and been immersed in since childhood, through my adult years, to the trophy podium and the World Cup finals.

I am so comfortable in this football world, so familiar with it and the direction of the journey, that I talk to these people the same way I would my players. I paint the same pictures, deliver the same messages, along the way making them realise that I am in total control of this project and they needn't worry. Their hands aren't required on the tiller. They realise their assistance is welcome, and needed from time to time, but their hands are not on the tiller. On that apparatus there is only room for me. I assure them that they can have faith in their appointment and that I'll deliver the project as planned. That is the way I roll.

That's what scuppered the takeover of Brisbane Roar by mining magnate Clive Palmer. The Roar owners had fought hard and done admirably to keep the club afloat after the original licence-owners hit hard times. Their contribution is etched in stone, but the time had come for them to move on and relinquish the club's licence. One of Australia's wealthiest men, Clive Palmer, held the A-League licence to the now defunct Gold Coast United. Palmer had been targeted by the FFA as the replacement owner of the Brisbane Roar. As coach of the team, I was summoned to a meeting with Palmer to discuss his plans for the club.

Sitting in his house, the voluminous figure of Clive Palmer was rocking back in his chair. I was sitting opposite him with Claude Baradel. Palmer shifted in his seat. 'I want to buy the Brisbane Roar,' he said, pulling out a crumpled piece of paper from his pocket. 'And here are the players you are going to take from Gold Coast. Scott Higgins, Kristian Rees, the Brazilian . . .' There were other players listed too, but at that point I couldn't get past the fact that he was telling me to take a player whose name he couldn't exactly recall.

'Now, I want you to write down your list of the players at Brisbane you'd like to keep and we'll make a team.'

I found myself just staring at him, a mix of astonishment and bemusement. I think I successfully disguised my total incredulity. Finally, I mustered a response. 'With all due respect, Clive, that's not how I coach. There's no collaboration with anyone. I do it my way. If you want to buy the Roar that's fantastic, but if you're the new owner and I'm going to be the coach, I'm not going to work that way. That is not how I do things.'

'What do you mean? I'm buying the club. I'm the owner. I talk with Miron [Bleiberg, the Gold Coast United coach] all the time.'

So I told him that he would, in that case, probably

need Miron to be his coach at his new club too. I told him I wasn't going to work in that environment but that if he wanted to buy the club and be successful, I would happily steer that ship for him. But there would be no collaboration between me and him on matters of football. Football was my business, mining was his business. The two wouldn't mix.

The meeting ended. I made my point, he'd made his. Palmer decided to pull out of the deal.

Not long after that meeting – it was about half an hour or so – FFA CEO Ben Buckley was on the phone to me, in a mild panic. 'Ange, what the hell did you say to Clive Palmer?' I emphasised that I hadn't said anything bad, but that if Palmer wanted to buy the club, and the FFA wanted Palmer to buy the club, then I wasn't going to be the coach. Not if he expected collaboration on football matters. It was pretty simple. 'But,' Buckley continued, 'the whole deal was predicated on you being the coach.' I apologised but suggested that, in that case, Buckley should have worded me up, or prepared me for the meeting in some way. Although in the end, the outcome would have been the same. Palmer's acrimonious exit from the A-League soon thereafter only served, in my mind, to vindicate the line I'd taken. There was simply no way I could have worked in that environment. It would have been a disaster.

Alternatively, I could have thought that, if this rich

and powerful guy was going to take over the club, I should position myself for some job security. Just tell him what he wants to hear, play along a little and secure my place. But that has never been the way I've conducted myself and I couldn't start then, even if it meant I was again going to be out of work soon. I reckon if I'd done that, somewhere in Palmer's mind he would have lost respect for me anyway. I had a very clear line of demarcation; these people's success and status and personal standing were one thing, but football is my realm and it is to be respected, and protected. If my boundaries are flexible and my borders porous, I can't be strong inside my football world, in front of my players and in the face of enormous on-field competition. That's no way to run a secure operation.

While I clearly mark my football territory, I have the utmost respect for the contribution of Frank Lowy. It's just over a decade since 2003's Crawford Report into the governance of Australian football, and the renaissance that followed, and I don't believe we as a game could have gotten where we are without Frank Lowy. The journey would have been a whole lot more problematic. I don't know of anyone in the initial stages who had the real clarity of purpose about what the game needed that he and John O'Neill had. O'Neill was such an effective lieutenant in the process. He is a formidable administrator and corporate figure in his own right, a former head of the NSW State Bank and CEO of the Australian Rugby Union. And Lowy gave the game this incomparable gravitas and access and credibility and status and passionate energy. He's done a lot for Australia and the country is way better for it. To my mind, the mark he has left on football will be his greatest gift.

I was still coach of the national youth teams at the time of Lowy's re-entry to football, so I was in and around the organisation a lot. I remember the focus in the office on establishing the new professional league, the A-League, and the push for membership in Asia and qualification for the World Cup. The office was all-consumed. The leadership was driven. The whole organisation was like it was on a war footing. There was no deviation, only complete focus.

Given my history in the NSL, I was included in poring over some of the club submissions for the new A-League, so I had a pretty good vantage point. The chairman was lobbying the government to get the funding that would enable everything to happen. There was such clarity of purpose and responsibility. I can't think of anyone else who would have delivered that combination, access to financial support and a laser focus on what was required to re-establish football and point it towards a bright future. Other candidates, I think, would have stagnated when faced with some matter or other. It took Lowy's leadership and the team he assembled to cut through everything, not getting bogged down in politics or detail. They had people to sift through the minutiae. Nothing would have been achieved were it not for the example the leadership were setting.

This is a good lesson. Change can be effected speedily if the message is clear and there is a really sharp point on the end of your message, in your objective. That sharpness will actually lance the obstacles that you confront, if the belief is strong and its point is maintained. The results can be amazing. You can cut through anything in next to no time. People will respond and mountains can be moved.

If the product is great too, which the A-League is, the achievements can be grand. Remember that we're talking about football here. It's not as if we were trying to sell something that people didn't want or didn't know about. Putting great ideas and energy around something like football, which is already fantastic, means big things can be achieved quickly. But even then, getting distracted or bogged down can result in a loss of focus and effectiveness. Direction can be lost. There are constantly issues in sport, in football. There have been plenty for the national body to deal with lately, and there'll always be more. Hours and hours are spent discussing them, momentum is lost.

I think back to the formation of the A-League and imagine how time-consuming the processes and discussions might have been, dealing with NSL clubs that weren't going to be part of the new competition. I remember that was overcome through total tunnel vision about what was required and how it was going to be achieved. If there's a lack of progress at any point along the journey it's probably because that focus has been diverted.

Of course those early days were brutal. Perhaps some of it unnecessarily. Maybe the focus was so intense that there wasn't the empathy to realise how harsh the new era seemed to some people. Frank Lowy would have been aware of some of the sensitivities because he'd come from the world of the NSL and football clubs. I don't think John O'Neill knew the hornets' nest he'd disturbed. He probably thought the game was already dead so there was nothing to kill. This new way was the only hope for a future, people just had to like it or lump it. I think now there's been the realisation that a lot of good people were treated pretty shabbily. Many who'd put so much selfless work into their love and passion were cast aside. I don't think there was an appreciation of what a resource they were, and still are. One of the big things about Frank Lowy was that he did understand all those things, because he came from that world. He was prepared to wear the consequences because he knew what was required. An omelette can't be made without breaking eggs but perhaps others should have mopped up after him.

Putting people in charge with no connection to the past enabled them to make unemotional decisions. That whole process showed me that, when the ingredients are right, big things can be achieved in a short space of time. The problems that we have from time to time – whether to expand the competition for example – are secondary to the belief in the whole project. Or they should be. The leadership must remain focused.

The principles of what Lowy did with the game's administration apply equally to what I do in my dressing room with my players. The correlation is total. The football field and the ninety minutes of play is a more acute environment, with time pressure. The beauty of sport is that in a very short space of time, all themes and messages are crystallised on the field of play. There is nowhere to hide. What you stand for is on show for all to see. The methods you employ are exposed to instant judgement. Players don't have the luxury of considering things. Time is truncated to the period between the referee's whistle starting and ending the game. Everything comes down to the myriad split-second decisions made under pressure during that time. Eager opponents are putting their own case to the test, testing yours, and, at the end, your team has to come through, true to its journey. A split second to react is all the players have, and they do so in the face of enormous intensity and physical pressure. It's in those moments that you see exactly what you've got. If they waver or persevere. And if there is any influence on them other than you and your message there is the possibility that they'll lose their edge. That is why I control the environment. When the heat's on during the game their default positions must not be confused. They must hear only one inner voice. If others off the field have been allowed to dip their oar in then I can't be sure which messages the players are operating from when under that pressure.

The answer to those questions will be a pointer to a team's success over time. While there isn't the same pressure, the same is true off the field. The administration has time to consider and plan but the impulses are the same, the internal battles are the same; whether they stick to the plan and push ahead or glance sideways and lose focus. Whether they are centred on the message or their attention gets dragged to the periphery. The former is a recipe for success, the latter leads to failure.

Working for the mega powerful and looking at different success stories – business, politics, military, sport – has only reinforced those views and lessons. Clarity of purpose has a huge impact, at any level. I had my doubts about the A-League initially. I wondered if it would work.

I remember the state of Melbourne Victory before the first season. The ownership group had just got up and running. They limped along at the start, finding it difficult to get traction and investment, a pale imitation of the club they have since become. There was a business function ahead of that first season to which I was invited. I thought it would be interesting to go, wondering what sort of people would be there. I remember at the time the South Melbourne and Melbourne Knights people were pooh-poohing the whole idea, they weren't going to go, that sort of talk. A the Crown Casino in Melbourne I rode the escalator up to the function and, as I got to the top, I was confronted with a sea of people. I thought I was in the wrong place. And then I started seeing some familiar faces, football people. I was overcome by the number of people in the room. I texted my wife Georgia and said that I thought this was actually going to be quite big. I couldn't really believe it, there were people attending from every club I'd encountered during the NSL era. That's when it dawned on me that the A-League was going to be a success. I knew the game but hadn't seen this happening. Having been away a lot with the Young Socceroos I hadn't had my finger on the pulse during that period. Lowy and O'Neill saw the possibility, or maybe they didn't, but they just knew that this league had to be created.

I remember Lowy fronting a press conference around the time the A-League launched. He answered a question about how confident he was the league would work. 'It will work if you come. I hope fans will come. I believe fans will come. They have to come.' And they did, they have.

Vision, leadership and necessity made it happen. They had the right ingredients. There was a broad love for the game so fans didn't have to be made from nothing. There were now the resources and the clout to properly drive the game's commercial needs. Think about it for a moment: the game went from being broke, having a woeful reputation with those in the corridors of power and industry, to starting a new fully professional league complete with a television partner. That is, from a starting point of no competition at all to an eight-team league in the blink of an eye. That was the result of vision and commitment and drive.

I draw on that type of thing as I set my team to take on the world's best players. The parallels are stark. Like my players, the game wasn't starting from nothing. Football had been around and was loved by many people. I believe there are many more people who love the game but are yet to be engaged. They will be part of this when the game grows bold again, but not before. When the vision becomes clear again, when people can see where they're being taken, only then will they come along on the journey in the numbers imagined, and needed. Football is big enough to absorb more growth, to embrace a broader vision.

On the field we talk about parking the bus, where a coach sets a team out to defend in numbers and not expose themselves to a superior opponent. If I'd taken that approach with the Socceroos, we'd have gone nowhere. If Frank Lowy had opted to park the bus, the game wouldn't have had even a fraction of the success it's enjoyed. So the message is clear. Crank up the engine and get going because the big results are only achieved by playing a power game.

7

LEAVE AND CLEAVE

After a century and a half of mainly British immigration, Australia's population make-up is changing. Multiculturalism is morphing from policy into practice. Asia is on the rise; its growing middle classes are altering the world's pivot points of politics and finance. Football is moving with the times in these parts of the world, too.

Establishment Australia, 'white-bread' Australia, 'WASP' Australia, 'old' Australia – whatever you call it – can no longer ignore the things that have been marginalised for generations. I'm referring to attitudes and not skin colour or ethnic profile here. And, until recently, Australia's sporting history has been a convenient exercise in celebration of everything but football. It's as if football didn't exist and that, prior to World War II and the beginning of large-scale European migration, it didn't have any meaningful place.

Contrary to popular belief, football has been played in Australia for as long as any other form of organised football. Until recently it had been widely accepted that the first game of football played in Australia was in 1880, in Parramatta, between the King's School and a team that called themselves the Wanderers. That has since been consigned to the bin. It seems football, as it resembled 'the association game', was in evidence as early as 1850. The expectation is that even earlier records will be uncovered.

It's important to stake a claim. Sydney University's rugby crest has '1863' emblazoned proudly upon it, which is interesting given that the Rugby Football Union didn't codify its rules until 1871. Possibly it's the case that the football game being played at Sydney University before codification resembled the game they played at The Rugby School in England. Meanwhile, Melburnians were busy organising their own football game, Australian Rules, which got underway in 1858. Given this backdrop, it's always seemed a bit strange that the 'association game' didn't break cover in Australia until 1880, and now we know that wasn't the case.

Some of Australia's oldest still-extant sports clubs are 'association' football clubs. Balgownie Rangers (1883) and Corrimal (1891) are still going strong in the Illawarra region, meanwhile Wallsend (1887), Adamstown (1889), West Wallsend (1891) and Edgeworth (1892) are all still prominent parts of the Newcastle sporting community. While my upbringing and experience in football were largely through the prism of ethnicity, it has become clear, to anyone who really wants to look, that football in Australia has a much deeper place in our history than the struggles of belonging of post-World War II migrants.

Belonging is never far from the football discussion. The game struggled to 'belong' in the formative colonial years, where other sports were embraced by the elite of the day and their settler mentality, sports like rowing and cricket and rugby. The process was, I think, exacerbated early on, as the press began to develop its relationship with sport. To this day the media is a mechanism that consolidates a hierarchy of acceptability and cultural appropriateness, determining the sports we celebrate and those we don't.

And then when the wogs came, people like my dad, that removed all doubt that football was foreign. From the very beginning, football has had to survive without the support of the top end of town. When it comes to covering football, race and ethnicity are probably the most written about topics there are. They have a centrifugal force, whirling around the thematic axis of belonging.

But the tide has definitely turned. Apart from the game being played by so many people, the sport is now recognised and acknowledged more. The success of the Socceroos and the appeal of the A-League are big reasons for this. The work of Frank Lowy and his team has cajoled a more supportive and empathetic view of football out of those who used to think differently.

I think that means Australia is now at a crossroads; the place where our historical sporting practices meet the nation's future needs. The choice confronting Australia is not about turning right or left, it's about deciding either to forge ahead into the opportunity that awaits or to drop anchor and stay where we are.

In order to bring corporate Australia along, football had to present its best face. A bright and new future had to be portrayed, one that was free of the byzantine way of doing business that had come before. By and large, the A-League has served that purpose well. Its inauguration was simultaneously powerful and polarising. Some people thought it was too brutal in its whitewashing of the sport's history, consigning many of the communities that had supported football to irrelevance. Others viewed the process as necessary. The tag line of the marketing campaign was 'It's football, but not as you know it'. Then CEO John O'Neill made the clear demarcation between 'old soccer' and 'new football'. In a world where slogans reign supreme, that one was top notch. The net effect was that football took off on a new corporate trajectory, with federal government backing, and scored goals that used to be frustrations and pipedreams, such as World Cup qualification and membership in the Asian Football Confederation.

Without being nearly the finished article, the A-League has shown how an organism can change to meet the challenges that present themselves. As football changed in order to make itself relevant to Australia, for want of a better way of putting it, it is now football that is asking the same thing of Australia. That the country change to become more relevant to its region and the world.

In 2004, as CEO of the FFA, John O'Neill set about breaking the chains that bound the sport. And his is an interesting story. He came with no emotional baggage or attachments, so ripping up football and starting again was relatively easy for him. Indeed, his professional and sporting history had him coming from the establishment side of the fence. He says he didn't come into football as a fan of the game but, by his own account, he certainly finished his tenure as one. He recognised through personal experience the immense power and reach of the game. John O'Neill might represent the journey that Australia as a country has to take. The question is whether Australia is ready and if it has the capacity to adjust, to move into this future. The signs suggest that some struggles remain.

If you've heard it once, you've heard it a thousand times; Asia is the reality of 21st-century Australia. Former Prime Minister Paul Keating said, while in office, that Australia needs to find its security in Asia, not from Asia. Part of that process involves building bridges into Asia. There have been many hints at policy direction regarding our roles and relationships within Asia and how important they are for us as a nation. For many countries in our region sport is the easiest access point. When it comes to the Subcontinent, our cricket commonality serves us well. But for the rest of Asia, we seem stumped, although we shouldn't be. Resoundingly, the answer is football. I feel almost foolish for stating something that bleeding obvious. On the matter of Asia and Australia and football, we've shown we have a long way to go before we're at the point, as a country, of really living up to Keating's exhortation or delivering on the policy papers churned out by the Canberra bureaucracy.

We only have to look at Prime Minister Malcolm Turnbull's April 2016 visit to China, where he led what was reported as the largest-ever trade mission to China. One thousand business leaders accompanied the PM and a collection of his cabinet members to the week-long event in China. Of course there is nothing unusual or wrong about this. However, when it was announced by the AFL that it intended to host a match in China between Port Adelaide and Gold Coast Suns, the prime minister couldn't help but clamber all over the possibilities, exalting the greatness of Australia's native game. If a prime minister, on behalf of a trade mission and business leaders, is going to impress the Chinese in the world of sport, surely he should use a sport common to both, like football, where Australia and China actually have relations and that the Chinese actually care about.

Neither the PM nor anyone in his office noticed that Chinese President Xi Jinping is actually a football fan. That around the same time as the trade mission he was outlining his plans for football in China, plans that involve investing billions of dollars, hosting the FIFA World Cup, building the Chinese professional league, opening 22000 football-specific high schools and working towards winning the FIFA World Cup in 2050. All this after Australia had hosted the Asian Cup only a year earlier, during which the Socceroos played China in the quarter-finals. As winners of the Asian Cup, it might have been prudent to celebrate this most unifying of Asian events. And with a group of Socceroos, including Tim Cahill, playing their club football in China (as beneficiaries of the huge investment being ploughed into the league), it didn't occur to anyone that having Socceroos as part of the trade mission might have been advantageous. Not to boast, but to share our sporting stars with China. The problem is that our players are bigger stars in the eyes of China than they are in ours. With whom might President Xi have preferred a photo, Timmy Cahill or Gary Ablett Jr?

The subtext to all this is that Australia strives to get from China more business, to open more markets and trade, attract more tourists and more students, but only so long as they swap their traditions and culture for real enlightenment, which thankfully for them is soon to arrive in the form of the AFL. It's staggering. Any official worth his or her salt would know the primacy of sport in the hierarchies of the Chinese communist party. Even more so with football under Xi Jinping.

There are other areas where we still have to make up ground. It's why I complain about things like play-ing surfaces in Australian stadiums. At the Asian Cup the Socceroos played against China at Brisbane's Lang Park (Suncorp Stadium). It is one of Australia's best stadiums, no question. But the playing surface that day would have endangered a herd of goats. It sends an incredibly bad message of our attitude towards the tournament we were hosting. It shouldn't have been so.

This is Asia's biggest thing, the Asian Cup, and we can't even get the grass right. For a match, incidentally, that was going to attract a monumental television audience in China. Their team was resurgent and the interest over there was massive. China is one of our major trading partners and perhaps the key consideration for Australian foreign policy going into the early phase of this new century. And we can't grow the grass we need, during a Brisbane summer, to play them in a game of football. Go figure.

The same went for our World Cup qualifying match against Tajikistan in Adelaide in 2016. The national team of Australia was going to Adelaide for an important game, and hadn't played a match in the South Australian capital for a decade. The venue was the city's new home, the redeveloped Adelaide Oval. Again, though, the playing surface was not international quality. The field looked pock-marked on television. The organisers had had six months to get it right.

Hosting the Socceroos and attracting a crowd to a venue that was redeveloped principally for Aussie Rules and cricket was only done to justify the hundreds of millions of dollars of public money spent on those other sports. And where was the infrastructure legacy for football, for Adelaide United or the grassroots? Football brings these big nights but they seem to yield little ongoing benefit. Surely that has to change.

It continued with the visit of Greece in June 2016, to play two friendlies in Sydney and Melbourne. I couldn't contain myself any longer. I thought the playing surface at the Olympic Stadium in Sydney was very poor. I said as much and actually expressed my embarrassment. My comments rankled some people, which wasn't necessarily the intention. But if nothing gets said, nothing gets done. For our nation to make progress we have to deal with the elephant in the room. It's groundhog day. To play this game properly, to an international standard, the playing surface has to be good. The image we portray of ourselves internationally is reflected by the facilities we provide. We let ourselves down when television pictures of poor pitches, with advertising markings from the NRL game the week before, are being beamed into overseas lounge rooms.

I don't raise this to pre-empt my team underperforming. To get the excuses in first, as it were. I speak to these issues because they scream at me about the lack of readiness of Australia to embrace football and the future it offers. Field preparation is an expression of ignorance, a lack of respect, or both. Neither is acceptable given the crossroads at which Australia finds itself.

The television numbers for the 2015 Asian Cup were impressive, again reinforcing how important it is to get these relationships right, and our house in order, so that we can better become part of Asia and live up to our own rhetoric. In China, the cumulative television reach for the Asian Cup, up until the semi-final stage, was 950 million people. That is, people who watched at least one minute of a match. Those are the same sort of metrics used in Australia and they determine where large broadcast rights fees and advertising dollars go. And whichever way you cut those numbers, they are bloody huge.

In South Korea, the team we played in the final, the audience figure for their semi-final was 18.2 million people. That's 37 per cent of their population. One might reasonably imagine the viewership for the final was even higher. And in Japan, the pre-tournament favourites who were eliminated by the United Arab Emirates, that quarter-final was watched by 21 million people – 17 per cent of its population. These are three of our largest trading partners, and a lot of their eyeballs were fixed on Australia in January 2015. The final itself was watched by in excess of 1 billion people around Asia. That's Monopoly money amounts, only it's not a game.

Australia's television numbers were significant too. The free-to-air telecast of the final earned the ABC their biggest audience share since the launch of digital television. The ticket sales across the tournament exceeded expectations, with 650 000 spectators attending matches, well above the target of 500 000. Local Asian communities rallied behind the teams of their heritage and it made for an unforgettable month of football.

To win it was amazing, at least for us. We didn't hear much more than a peep from officialdom. There was certainly no mention of a reception with the prime minister or anything like that, even though its standard fare when the netball or cricket or rugby teams win. This isn't sour grapes from me. I don't really care if I ever see the inside of Kirribilli House. But it does say a lot about where we're at. The Western Sydney Wanderers winning the Asian Champions League also went through to the keeper, so we weren't alone. The penny will only drop on how big these achievements are when Australia has embraced its position in the world, using football as a key way of doing it.

The failed bid to host the 2022 FIFA World Cup also shone a light on the struggle Australia is having with its identity. Hindsight is a wonderful thing, so it's easy to say that it was a folly to presume we had a serious chance to win the hosting rights. The scorn has only increased following the scandals that have engulfed FIFA after that voting process. However, at the time, the attempt to take Australia to this level of international consideration was supported by the government to the tune of $45 million. It was completely in keeping with the energy and positivity of the Lowy era. The FIFA shenanigans and ensuing fallout are one thing. The other, relevant to this discussion, is the manner in which local vested interests attempted to derail the effort through their fear and intransigence.

One may have expected Australia's sporting community to fall in behind the attempt to snare the world's biggest sporting event, the World Cup, as it has done for Olympic Games campaigns. Australia loves a mega event and has done them very well. However, the national drive to showcase ourselves and host the world wasn't as forthcoming when it came to the World Cup. Officials in the NRL and particularly in the AFL went into paroxysms at the thought of their winter competitions being interrupted in order to accommodate it. Unable to acquiesce and support such a nation-building opportunity, rival sports and their media lackeys ran in opposition to the campaign. I remember a front page story about the World Cup bid, accompanied by a photo of Aussie Rules great Ron Barassi puncturing a (round) football with his bare hands. It was a quasi-Godzilla pose and scowl, the subtext something like 'the might of Aussie Rules will see off the barbaric hordes of the football World Cup'.

Unfortunately that wasn't an isolated example. Notwithstanding the scandalous and corrupt voting system at FIFA, it's hard to imagine the world awarding the hosting rights to its most precious event to a country so obviously opposed to it. As far as we were concerned, the message was very clear: the Olympics are a worthy pursuit for Australia but football will be resisted.

Yet it's not just the detractors who can't or won't see football, Asia and the future. There are too many in football who choose to look away. This nervous, insecure mentality revealed itself when Massimo Luongo was nominated for the Ballon d'Or (Golden Ball), awarded to the world's best player. Rather than shout Mass's listing from the rafters I got the sense that Australia almost apologised for it, was embarrassed for him to be on the same long-list as Lionel Messi and Cristiano Ronaldo. *How could Massimo be on that list? It must be a mistake.* We should have celebrated that, held him up as someone notable and his nomination as something noteworthy. Instead there was the feeling that we couldn't wait for the whole episode to blow over. But no one had lobbied for his inclusion on the list. He was nominated on the strength of his crowning as the best player of the Asian Cup in 2015. A tournament held every four years, it is Asia's footballing pinnacle. Mass Luongo was deemed the best player in that prestigious tournament, and Australia was embarrassed by it. By extension, it seems implicit that we are embarrassed by Asia and the Asian Cup. It's going to be pretty difficult to fully realise everything the Asian Century needs to be for Australia if we are embarrassed by it and its most popular sport. And we mustn't delude ourselves that Asia didn't notice.

I see the way Australia reacts to football. In my mind there's no point dancing around the topic. Australia as a country is like the teenager who is struggling with their identity. Until now the country has done what it thought its parent(s) – Great Britain and the Commonwealth – wanted it to do. But now, the future is opening up in a whole new direction, and the growing pains are distinct.

I see the role of the national team as integral to changing this mentality. We don't like to be the smallest dog in the fight, really. We tell ourselves we love being the underdog but our treatment of football exposes a different truth. If we've got a chance we'll have a go, afterwards telling everyone how brave we are and how we love the underdog. There is rarely a bigger underdog in Australian sport than its national football team, the Socceroos, playing on the world stage. But down the years, other than from football fans, there's been no love or determination to win that fight. Thankfully the people of Australia are realising in greater and greater numbers just what the equation is and support for the Socceroos has grown. On game day the sense of national pride in the stadium is palpable. As you travel, you notice the number of Aussie backpackers who now proudly wear their Socceroos replica shirts. In the past people might have turned up to a Socceroos match in a Wallabies jersey or a one-day cricket shirt. It's significant that people are proud enough, and connected enough, to wear Socceroos paraphernalia. It wasn't always so and it's a sign of the shifting times.

One wonders what sort of place Australia would be if we hadn't had this resistance to football, whatever the historical reasons for that. Imagine the speed with which post-war migrants would have been absorbed into Australian society if football had been organised better and respected more, if there were established leagues and clubs in which they could have participated. I have to hope that's of some benefit to migrants arriving today. I think of promising young Australian players like Awer Mabil, who began playing football in a Kenyan refugee camp, and Mustafa Amini, whose father fled war-torn Afghanistan. But I also think of all those who have come to Australia, through whatever circumstance, and found belonging, community and recognition in following the A-League or playing in a better-developed amateur football system.

If that had been the case seventy years ago perhaps

we'd be further down the track of engaging with Asia and the world, rather than taking the baby steps we are now. It was hardly the fault of the new arrivals that this wasn't the case, yet they were pilloried for forming their own clubs and playing their own game. They were criticised for being exclusive. In fact the opposite was the case, football and the clubs they built allowed them to form connections, to find inclusion as they settled and formed Australian communities. If Australia had football as a welcome post for new arrivals, migrants mightn't have needed to ghettoise themselves, as many did, with the attendant problems, in order to make sense of this place.

Now making sense of Asia is the pressing challenge. Being welcoming of Asia is a big part of that. It must start with things like allowances for Asian players in the A-League. There are many Asian leagues that have special visa dispensation for Asian players as part of their foreign-player quotas. The A-League doesn't. If Australian football wants Australian society to take Asia and football more seriously then it should lead the way. Allowing A-League clubs an additional Asian visa player would show the rest of Asia that we're in this with them, that we value them. Presently the A-League allowance is for five visa players, with no specific stipulation for players from Asia. At the time of writing, there are no Asian visa players in the A-League. This has to be corrected, as a matter of policy, particularly when you consider the AFC Champions League, which is such a big thing for our clubs. In that competition only three visa players can be listed, so two foreigners from the regular A-League squad might have to miss out, but an Asian player can be added as a fourth foreigner. If football in Australia wants the benefits of Asian membership, then it has to also endorse Asian football. The same equation faces the country in general. We can't pick and choose, the relationship can't be one of convenience. It must be symbiotic.

I am impatient for that to happen and I believe that, in time, it will. The forces of politics and trade and the sheer weight of people will ensure that it does. Any team I coach is going to do their bit to make that happen too. I won't rest, and I won't let my players rest either, in the pursuit of that goal. That is the gift that awaits Australia; becoming a seriously meaningful player in Asia and the world's most pervasive cultural, sporting, political and financial movement. I want to contribute to this awakening as Australia's national coach. I'll have probably two World Cup campaigns to make those inroads. Then I'll have to do it as an Australian coach in a major European league. Not a Greek-born Aussie – as if that would give it more legitimacy – but as an Australian coaching in big-time club land. That is the journey.

I know that the Socceroos are up for that challenge. All the players have travelled across the globe. Many of them have settled overseas to pursue their career. Everywhere they've gone, they've found football front and centre. They know what it means to people around the world. They want that for Australia and its people too. They believe it can happen and that they can be a key conduit. That is a powerful motif. They want to be the latest part of the solution for Australia. The journey that began with the Socceroos' first attempt to qualify for the World Cup in 1966 and was kicked along by the 1974 Socceroos, as well as by those who've followed.

In the meantime, and while we prepare that gap to be bridged, football provides Australia with its best full-length mirror. There is no sport that better sums up the journey of Australian society, highlights its contradictions and prejudices, as well as encapsulating its possibilities. It is not spleen-venting to suggest such things and to make note of the opposition the sport has faced. It illustrates how Australia's current position in the world, and the crossroads it faces, is manifestly more challenging because of its obscured relationship with football and that historical-cultural blind spot. Because football was ignored, relatively, and because Australian sport indulged parochialism, myopia ensued. The view to the future has been blurred. But the winds of change are blowing and that fog will disperse. There will be a clear and brilliant view to Australia's Asian future. And in that future, the ball Australians will be chasing as it bounces along to the pot of gold at the end of the rainbow will be a round one.

8

NO-MAN'S-LAND

Cultural cringe has had a big impact on football's development in Australia. It still does. The subconscious attitude even among some football people is of inferiority; that whatever happens here is somehow second rate, held with a 'that's not how they do it in Europe' sort of sneer. Its adherents hover above and around the game with an unwelcome ubiquity, dropping ignorant waffle as they feel like it, muddying the waters and hindering progress. Football's actualisation would be achieved in next to no time with the unqualified support of all those who profess their love for the game. The reasons why football fans would choose to sit on the sidelines and snipe at the Australian incarnation would probably provide enough material for an entire conference on the sociology of sports.

We see evidence of it bobbing up around finals time every A-League season, when the cry comes out from some to revert to a first-past-the-post league champion. That is the way other football leagues around the world do it so it must be the true measure. There is an annual failure to acknowledge that the champion in Australia has been decided by the winner of the grand final for decades, including in the NSL. That the finals series is hugely successful also escapes attention. The fact that Europe may do well to adopt the play-off system to enhance their own competitions probably doesn't get the traction it might. The autumnal carping about the finals, arriving with metronomic precision, is interminably infuriating. And if it's not the finals series, it'll be something else people pick at. In isolation the issues are nothing, really, but combined they speak of disunity.

It would be bad enough if this inferiority complex was propagated by people outside the game. The tragedy, to my way of thinking, is that it holds frightening currency inside the game. I fear that the game's adherents have become so used to being beaten over the head about football's shortcomings that they've started to believe the malevolent stuff that's been hurled at the game over the years. Inexplicably, football is so willing to self-flagellate. The self-loathing has reached such intensity that the sport lashes itself to within an inch of its life, its raw flesh dangling and dripping.

And so it is from beneath this backdrop that, as the men's Olympic team, the Olyroos, failed to qualify for the Rio Olympic Games, the gnashing of teeth reached deafening levels. Again. There can be no question there's a gap in our development system but I find the vacuity of the discussion breathtaking.

Coach Graham Arnold's Olyroos were the last men's team to qualify for the football tournament at the Olympics. In making it to the Beijing Games of 2008, Arnold's team had to progress through the Asian Football Confederation, the first time this was required for that age group. It was an arduous journey, where success was ultimately only achieved on the last day of qualifying, on a frozen artificial pitch in Pyongyang in North Korea. It was hardly the most hospitable place for such a defining game, but the Olyroos won the day and secured their place in the Olympic tournament. The achievement is even more noteworthy considering the fact that the NSL had been in decline up until its closure in 2004 and in the intervening time there had been no focus on youth or a youth league. The A-League itself had only started in August of 2005. There were scant opportunities for eligible young players to get regular football. It was, in development terms, a black hole. There have been two subsequent campaigns – for

London 2012 and Rio 2016 – led by Aurelio Vidmar, and both have ended in failure.

The fallout of the failure and the so-called analysis is the same each time. There's no awareness that in a global context the game has changed at youth level and that the reference points we used to have are no longer realistic. We were once very successful at the men's youth level, as measured by qualification for youth tournaments and then progression through those tournaments. There is a line of thought that we should still be making the same progress. But we are now on a divergent path. Firstly, we left Oceania, which makes for more difficulty, itself a welcome thing. Furthermore, the investment in youth football throughout Asia compared to ours is staggering. We look at things with the perspective of the successful days of yore, but times have changed.

As an example, through the 1980s and '90s in particular, most of our best young players were part of residential programs at the Australian Institute of Sport (AIS). The AIS was revolutionary. A multisport, government-funded and inspired venture that put Australian sport at the forefront of science and advancement. Football benefitted from this as well. The AIS, at its peak, dovetailed with the NSL, which was booming as a production line of talent in its own right. The opportunities for the best young players to play senior football were abundant. The AIS was leading the world in best practice and the NSL was a vibrant competition, at least on the field. It was an example of Australia at its best: innovative, boisterous, aggressive, positive, eager, self-determining.

The AIS is now in relative decline if one is to listen to the criticisms of Australian Olympic Committee boss, John Coates. But it had served notice of its effectiveness to the world, so the world came and copied it. Imitation is the greatest form of flattery so that is a feather in Australia's cap. With regard to football, there weren't many countries, and certainly none from Asia, who were taking youth development as seriously as that. European countries' youth focus was centred on the role clubs played in developing players. The national interest in supporting the youth level was scant.

South American countries, particularly Brazil and Argentina, had a more aggressive approach to youth football, which might have had something to do with targeting the international transfer market. FIFA youth tournaments were effective scouting opportunities for European clubs on the prowl for talent, much like how American sports and the AFL have draft combines. South America was a gold mine and its clubs derived significant revenue from the sale of its best young players to Europe. Africa, particularly sub-Saharan Africa, was prominent in youth tournaments but more as a function of those countries' seemingly bottomless pit of talent and inexhaustible passion for the game. You couldn't say that this subset of African football was at the cutting edge of youth development. Nevertheless, there was a gap in youth football globally and Australia found a creditable place therein through the combination of the AIS, the realities of the NSL and easy passage through the Oceania Confederation.

I'd venture to say then, and again comparatively, that we were investing in our best young talent. The financial model of the NSL, if one could attribute such grandiose corporate language to it, was also partly predicated on selling players to Europe. Indeed, some of Australia's biggest-ever player transfers were in the NSL era, selling players to European clubs. Mark Viduka, Zeljko Kalac and Brett Emerton were just three such players whose transfers provided enormous financial sustenance and stability for the Australian clubs involved, Melbourne Knights, Sydney United and Sydney Olympic respectively. There were others too, and it is only now, over a decade into the life of the A-League, that Australian clubs are getting anywhere near the fees paid for that generation of NSL players. In time those figures will be routinely surpassed, but those wheels are turning slowly.

To hail the Socceroos team of 2006 as the golden generation, you have to acknowledge that they were spawned from the NSL and/or the AIS program. This is the team that went to the round of sixteen in the 2006 World Cup in Germany, only to lose late in the game to a controversial penalty against the ultimate champions, Italy. While the country was euphoric about the achievement, and rightly so, there wasn't much reflection on the role the much maligned NSL had in the development of that talent. Let's correct that for the record here and now.

The culture around NSL clubs was committed and vibrant. The discourse about the game and the league was detailed and intricate, and that contributed to player development as much as coaches and training sessions did. Football is a language, and the NSL and its member clubs offered full immersion in it. There can be no doubting the nuanced quality of players it produced, like Josip Skoko, Mark Bresciano, Vince Grella, Scott Chipperfield, Brett Emerton, Jason Culina.

Getting the A-League started was bold, but we've dragged the chain on youth development. The league has some way to go before it can match its predecessor, the NSL, in developing vertically integrated clubs that cater for every level from kids right through to the professional senior team, all with the same colours and badge. Other countries have invested and powered ahead. We haven't and clearly we've plateaued, yet our historical success remains the reference point. We can't expect better results when, relative to our competitors, we have put less into the system. There are fewer opportunities for young players in senior football now, not more. This is purely on the basis of numbers and available positions.

The FFA has also reduced the National Youth League (NYL) – which took years to establish – to a very short summer season. Its eight-game duration, run concurrently with the A-League itself, is barely worth having. Part of the aim of a youth development program is to secure the optimal number of competitive games in a season, which is somewhere around forty games. The bulk of the games for that cohort are, I acknowledge, now played through winter in the National Premier League (NPL) competitions that have taken the place of the old state leagues. There the younger A-League players play against adults, which is a good thing. But when the NYL was established, and run at the same time as the A-League, it was to provide around twenty games over the A-League season. The idea was that the A-League youth teams would then transfer into the winter-time NPL competitions. The combination would provide the volume of matches required. Furthermore, aligning NYL squads with the A-League program also served to provide integration between the two, potentially enhancing the development experience for young players moving into the senior ranks.

The surgery performed on the NYL to reduce it to eight games, which really amounts to an amputation, was implemented on the basis of cost rather than program effectiveness. The problems have been further exacerbated in some instances by the political resistance from state-based NPL and member federations, hostile to having A-League teams playing in their competitions. Some antagonists' misgivings stem from the competitive instincts of NPL clubs, masked as deep suspicion that their existence is under threat. Others feel that their NPL operating model is made vulnerable when A-League youth teams play in their competitions, because at stake are league points that might determine whether they're relegated or survive. They also worry about access to the available playing talent. That there is such disagreement on an important issue points to very worrying fracture lines at the core of the game's structure.

Overlay all this with the diminished impact of the AIS, which now caters for players two years younger than when the program was at its zenith. The real picture of our dysfunctional youth system begins to emerge. It's simply not possible for us to be as competitive as we were.

I have to take issue with some historical analysis, too. The warm fuzzy feeling we got when the Young Socceroos were flying, or when the Olympic team qualified for the Barcelona Olympic Games via a final qualification win against Holland and a magical Ned Zelić performance. Even in those halcyon days I feel our focus was misguided. Team success shouldn't be the measure of the system's efficacy. It is a by-product, sure, but shouldn't be the goal. It doesn't *really* matter if we win the FIFA Under 20s World Cup. It might justify some bureaucratic budget line-item. It will feed the egos of a coach or two. The only thing that's noteworthy is that it might propel some of our young players to bigger and more demanding leagues. Otherwise, it is a diversion from the main game.

We were winning at youth level, comparatively speaking, but failing to qualify for the World Cup. I'd say that our need for vindication as a football country propelled the status of the youth teams. Their success made us feel better. More worthy. But if we have success-ful teams that don't produce world-class players, we've missed the point. That is evidence of a failed system: we haven't produced world-class players. In the 1980s and '90s one could argue that the bulk of the players were definitely international class. Their combination produced strong youth teams. In the twenty years since 1995, how many players have we developed where we could say, seriously, that they were world class? Youth football should be about producing the best possible players. The beneficiaries of this process should be the

Socceroos and the A-League. If the youth teams rise and fall but produce individuals of international quality, the system is working. If the youth teams succeed (whatever that means) but don't produce talent for the Socceroos and the A-League, the system is broken.

With respect to the current crisis at Olyroo level, a team that fails to qualify for the Olympics doesn't mean a failed system any more than a qualifying team means a functional system. The only measure has to be the quality of the individuals. Our harkening back to the old days is also a function of the fact that we found it too difficult to qualify for the World Cup proper. The Young Socceroos sated our desire for international recognition. They were our big deal. And it should be noted that the Young Socceroos' path to the FIFA tournaments was through Oceania, an altogether easier task. Thereafter, preparing teams for the final tournaments could be more focused and progression was more achievable. The Asian route tests our system more consistently and much earlier, it's only that the system has buckled under the examination.

Better players make better teams and better teams progress through tournaments. We've dismantled a youth system that produced players and now wonder why the teams are struggling. Asia is a bigger and more consistent test than Oceania was or could ever be. The results are coming in earlier now, in the qualification phase, whereas before we only got the teacher's report from the tournament itself.

In response to the gap that's emerged we have started the National Curriculum. We've had similar incarnations previously, and seemingly endless reviews of this and that. The curriculum provides a foundation and a framework for developing players and coaches. But when one of our youth teams fails to qualify for a tournament and people point to the curriculum as the source of that failure you know something has been lost in translation. Part of the curriculum is the Skillaroos program, the working title for which was Project 22. That refers to 2022, so we're still some years away from the program's maturation. We shouldn't refer to the curriculum as having failed us today when the project has only run half its course. We must measure it along the way, of course, and obviously qualification campaigns are part of that ongoing assessment, but the inclination from too many is to throw it all out.

When you consider the timelines, the current Olyroos and Under 20s (who also missed out on their world cup) shouldn't form the basis of the discussion because they are products of the years 1999–2005. That predates both the influx of Dutch coaches to senior coaching positions and the National Curriculum. We need to understand that tomorrow's footballers are being trained today and anything you get between now and then will be a bonus. The point is, in our hysteria, we mix up the issues and confuse the analysis. We throw the baby out with the bath water. Repeatedly. Simplistic commentary on complex issues serves nothing.

The most uncomplicated starting point is that there is no alignment within our system and other countries are investing vastly larger sums on developing players. In Asia, Australia wouldn't be among the top twenty spenders on youth football. Extrapolate that to a global measure and it's frightening to think where we rank. We don't invest enough cold hard cash, but that isn't the only answer. We need to be more disciplined in following a line of argument, in staying the course. I'm prepared to assume that when an option has been chosen and we begin implementing it, there is a clarity of vision as to what that is going to look like at its end point. Financial investment is required, but so too an investment in the process, via a disciplined adherence to the plan. Because there is no quick fix in football. The game is too difficult to master and the sport is too competitive. Australia seems to be exposed more to the false economy of a quick fix because of the domestic challenge from other sports.

Competitor countries aren't bound by the same perceived fight for survival and so seem to be more patient. Shareholder meetings every six months demand a return on investment – tournament qualification, in football's case – and preclude the football greenhouse's ability to germinate its seeds. The clamour for instant results means we cut our noses off to spite our face. Of course there is the possibility of quick international success in the rugby codes, because the competition is infinitesimal by comparison. And Aussie Rules has no international benchmark at all, so god knows how good we actually are or could be at that sport. Aussie Rules exists in an almost fully inflated bubble of entitlement, hubris and self-absorption, so football shouldn't compare itself to that sport. Let's face it, if Germany or Brazil, or god help us the USA, actually had a hundred serious years of Australian Rules Football history and desire and investment, Australia might not reign supreme even in a game of its own invention. Much like England's inability to dominate the game it was chiefly responsible for bringing to the world, football.

Unfortunately, the Australian football system has no patience. Australia is in a hurry, always, to be recognised globally. Such desire and ambition, if harnessed properly, can be a potent advantage. But as things stand, if we can't master something in a millisecond then we can't respect ourselves, let alone expect others to respect us. It's a cultural pincer movement that inhibits football's growth. Australians seem to have

unbridled aggression when it comes to proving themselves on the biggest stage while simultaneously shying
away from the examination provided by the international glare, skulking further into parochialism when
the competition gets too hot. Football reaffirms that
story. You can't bluff your way through football. You
can't survive in the world of football with a PR campaign and a compliant media and business sector. Any
impatience, negligence, ill-discipline or lack of coordination will expose the weak and unprepared. Australia
has been exposed. Australia has its pants down.

The problems we had fifteen years ago weren't add-
ressed fifteen years ago. We have mistakenly used our
youth teams as a development tool for coaches, not
young players. When something is in limited supply,
such as talented youngsters, the best coaches should
be assigned to their development. No risks should be
taken with them. Football battles for financial resources.
Football battles for athletic talent because of the opportunities presented by other sports. We don't have the
number of players at our disposal that we really need
to be consistently competitive. Therefore we must be
smarter and more focused with the playing resources we
do have. Do more with less. The available jewels are in
limited supply so hand them to someone who's not going
to be nervous holding them or drop them along the way,
before they can be delivered as the finished article.

We haven't done that. Instead we've used the youth teams as a tool to groom a coach thought to have potential. To develop the coach! An individual may have been successful coaching at senior level or may have just retired from a fruitful playing career, so we hand over the jewels. We install a rookie coach, one who may or may not have a propensity or desire for youth development, and we wonder why there are gaps. There are rough diamonds there, for sure, but we don't have coaches with the knowledge to polish them.

If we were serious, we'd have made the decision early that youth development requires specialised coaches. The higher up the chain a youth team is, the more experienced and specialised the coaching must be. We find ourselves light years away from that approach. There has to be a strand in the coach education system for specialists in youth development. It's a must. To date, coach education has been one size fits all, which is inadequate. It's impossible to progress if we identify something like this as a deficiency and yet, for the very next cycle, appoint another first-year coach to take charge of the group coming through. Then, if qualification isn't achieved, the process is deemed a failure. The failure was at the very beginning of the process, before we even started, because we failed to address the requirements of the job when considering the candidates. We talk about developing players but measure the system by teams winning or losing. It just doesn't make sense.

The real test of the system is the number of players who move to senior football and, when they get there, really shake the tree. How many can we point to who have done that in recent years? How many kids have we delivered to the pointy end of the game to give them games and growth? Not enough, I'd say. During the critical stages of development, has the game given them the experiences and the coaches needed? If questions such as these are asked at the start of the process there can be no other course of action than having development specialists in the coaching positions.

If specialised coaching is one thing, the low number of kids being prepared is another. We have the grand total of twenty kids, aged fifteen or sixteen, housed at the AIS, training full time. The rest of the potential talent has been cast into the hands of the club youth system, to the extent that it exists, and then we wonder why we are finding it tough to compete internationally. And the A-League clubs, the apex of football in Australia, haven't even had youth programs until recently. Developing talent is a numbers game and we are bringing a fantastically small number of chips to the table.

At the Olyroos qualifying campaign for Rio 2016, a competition held in Qatar, we were the only country without a single media representative covering our team. I find it embarrassing that there is no external interest or support for the tournament yet there is such bilious dissatisfaction with the results. I remember when I was playing in the national youth teams I sat next to journalists on the way to the tournament games. It's been forgotten that these tournaments have a status. Nowadays there's no importance attached to them, except when the team fails, then all hell breaks loose. Asia is a whole new ball game. Some of our very best youth teams from the past would probably have failed to qualify if they'd had to navigate the Asian conference we face now, particularly at its current point of evolution. Instead they strolled through Oceania qualification, did well at a tournament, and everyone thought everything was rosy. Going through Oceania you could have an off day and still get through. Not so in Asia. You get found out.

The discussion around the Olyroo campaign for Rio also troubled me. Much of the talk centred on the disruption it caused in the A-League and that players would have been better off at their clubs than playing for their country. Others talked about club coaches hiding or warehousing potential candidates by not selecting them so that they wouldn't be picked for the national team and go on to miss chunks of the A-League season. Has the view of our national youth teams' role really come to that? The concept that playing for your country is more important than anything else has been diluted.

We only seem to take interest once the results are in or when a player is missing club football. You don't hear about what was best for the players concerned, only the teams they play for. I have sat around tables with A-League coaches and heard it said that, if a player's selection was going to affect his club team, he didn't want him going with that national team. So the FFA finds itself having to force players to play for their country. That's incredibly damaging. At the very least it informs the players' subconscious that the national team is less important.

The dissolution of the NSL created a black hole in youth development. It was augmented by the commencement of the A-League – where youth development wasn't really a consideration, to start with – and by getting rid of so many people with history in the game, particularly coaching history. The move into football's brave new world left behind youth coaches who'd had twenty years of experience. They were cast aside. For the guys working in the trenches of the NSL and its youth league, there were no opportunities. When they were needed more than ever, to fill the hole in youth development and playing experiences that came with the transition from the NSL to the A-League, they were rendered useless. They were thought of as another part of a game that was rotten to the core and hopelessly dysfunctional. Too many were deemed culpable for that, it seems.

My sacking as coach of the national youth teams in 2007 highlights that fact. Maybe at the time I was let go because I was seen as part of 'old soccer'; a barnacle of the ethnic enclaves that bound the NSL together. Someone like me would only poison the new system because I was so inextricably linked with the old one. And the old hadn't work, apparently. So after seven years in the job as youth boss, doing what I now call my PhD in football coaching, I was released. All the knowledge I'd accumulated was just expunged.

My experience sums up the game's experience. I wasn't wanted at the time, I was part of the problem, but now I'm someone people want to engage. I haven't changed, others' views have. The really bizarre thing was that I was never more ready to do the youth job than when they sacked me and I couldn't have been less ready for the job than when I was initially hired. It was totally arse-about-face.

All to replace me with someone from overseas, who must have been better, because he wasn't Australian. Irrespective of the fact that this person would have nowhere near the experience that I'd accumulated. If it wasn't to be me there were other locals at the time who'd been in and around the set-up. But the choice was to go with a scorched-earth approach, razing everything and everyone to the floor.

The issue came into focus for me (again) when I was in France in 2004 with the Young Socceroos on a development tour. That group included Mark Milligan, Mark Bridge and Danny Vukovic, to name just a few. At the conclusion of the camp and after the players had departed for Australia, I remained in France with my assistant coach for the tour, Jean-Paul de Marigny. We spent some time together at Clairefontaine, French football's national institute. It's the French equivalent to AIS and is credited with the rise in French football's stock, culminating in the World Cup 1998 and Euro 2000 successes.

We happened to time our visit with an induction camp, from which a new intake of players would be selected. JP and I were eager to see the science behind the French selection system. I mean, they're producing the best players in the world so they must have some whiz-bang method of testing the kids to find the best among them. We actually discovered that the talent identification was fairly basic. Kids were asked to juggle a football and play a game. I looked across the sea of French kids, all of whom could have been the next big thing. Scouring this group of next-generation Patrick Vieiras and Thierry Henrys, I was hunting for that special thing. I was trying to see what they were looking for, almost squinting with concentration. There must have been some special thing that I could take back to Australia to turn our system around. That one tool that produces players of international quality. What were we looking at? What were we looking for?

I asked JP to translate the French conversation that was buzzing around us. There was an old French guy who as it turned out, along with Gérard Houllier, had been part of Clairefontaine since its inception. He was politely accommodating, but he was giving us nothing. I was badgering JP for information, who turned to me and said, agitated, 'He just knows.' I thought, *Bloody great. How am I going to take that back to Australia?*

But I believed him. He did just know. It's called experience. And after my seven years in that job I understood even better what it was he meant. What the best young players looked like and what their characteristics were. I knew as much as he knew. We both knew. The message for Australia is that there is no magic, single ingredient. We had the range of ingredients but, out of ignorance and lack of confidence, we'd gone about washing them down the plug hole, time and again. Our approach is to look for that one ingredient, but that one thing doesn't exist. And when we couldn't find what didn't exist, we nuked our knowledge bank.

We haven't valued experience in Australia. In fact, we've gone in the other direction; the longer you've been associated with the game the bigger a problem you're perceived to be. The essence of football hasn't changed. The ball is still round. The styles and emphases may vary, but the roots of the game remain the same. We have placed little store in that. We've tried to sterilise the process, distilling it into a series of 'measurables', like winning. That formula has been used to justify putting people with history on the scrap heap. It has done next to nothing to conjure a new way of developing players. We've wasted a lot of time, and people.

That old guy at Clairefontaine, he'd seen it all before and his knowledge was respected. Probably he couldn't transfer it into some binary code for software, because people can't be put into a box like that. But years of watching had taught him a lot, and that was respected. In Australia, on the other hand, we keep thinking there is some virtue in starting again and again. There isn't. If experience and historical reference aren't appreciated then mistakes will be repeated. The only people who can give a useful account of past approaches are the ones who were there, so the game was errant in dismissing their opinion just because they weren't considered part of today's world.

Adding to the scorched earth approach, and probably feeding it, is that the default position is to head

overseas for expertise. It's another example of us thinking there is a quick fix to our problems, that Australia
is the problem and something or someone from outside
will be able to wave their wand. As though that's all it
takes. Whatever is international flavour of the month
moves to the top of our list. The Dutch play attractive football so let's bring that out here. Germany has
won the World Cup, on the back of a ten-year plan, so
let's go German. The Belgians have a fantastic group of
players in the top leagues and are doing well, so let's go
Belgian. But all we are doing is painting over the cracks
in the system. Someone can't come in from another
country and understand why we're where we are at and
how things have changed (or not) over the decades. So
much time and money is spent getting these people to
a place where they can even vaguely understand the
issues, let alone getting them properly up to speed. I am
most certainly not against information, talent and ideas
from overseas, but I am totally against the fallacy that
we don't already have expertise like that available here.

Too often the starting point from foreigners is that
our players are rubbish and Australia has no football
culture. They're happy to buy into that and then perpetuate it. And too many Australians reinforce that
with sycophancy. I'm not sure if the game knows what
it's looking for, it's so sensitive to the marketing hype
of the English Premier League's highlight reels, so busy

longing for a European utopia. There is no real and discernible commitment to putting in place the principles and foundations that underpin the great football powers and their cultures, which we rightly admire from a distance. We lust after the curtains and wallhangings but pay no attention to the foundations. In established football markets, including but not limited to England and Europe, those foundations are adherence to a plan, a valuing of and pride in the local football knowledge and culture, and investment in infrastructure, leagues and facilities (including stadiums) that promote and support football.

For a long time our system has paid lip-service to building its coaching reservoir. There is a direct comparison here with the education system. It's generally accepted that, outside of their family, the single biggest influence on children's school experience is the quality of the teaching. It's so obvious it feels ridiculous to even say it, but exactly the same applies to football. Good coaching experiences will fuel football's fire at the grassroots and beyond. It means more players, and better players, and over time the performance of our national teams will improve. It's a pretty straightforward algorithm.

Meanwhile, Australian football has outsourced the vast bulk of its coaching responsibility to mum and dad volunteers who, out of love for family, community and football, have done an incredible job. I just find it difficult to believe that they are expected to carry such a burden for the game while at the same time, at the other end of the pyramid, the game laments the difficulties of international competition. I can't think of many, if any, of our international competitors who are so reliant upon (often but not always) untrained volunteers to establish our players' technical foundations. A qualification: I love Australian volunteerism. It speaks to something very special in the communities right across Australia. It is another thing altogether, however, for a sport to rely so heavily on that cohort and simultaneously expect international competitiveness to result.

The fact that football has such an incoherent schools policy exemplifies this. In many countries I've visited, the gaps in youth development between national federations and clubs are picked up by schools. I can't see that we've made any real progress in this direction whatsoever. Imagine the weight that could be lifted by having schools, with pools of teachers trained in football pedagogy, contributing to the process. The facilities in the schools system would also alleviate some of the problems we face with limited community access to playing fields. I struggle to understand how this isn't a burning priority for the game.

As all these issues cascade there appears to be more confusion. Simple questions are difficult to address, or even decipher. Can Australia identify its best three youth development coaches? Or its best three talent spotters? Has anyone studied the emergence of Aaron Mooy or Massimo Luongo or Tom Rogic or Trent Sainsbury? Who coached them and is their work worth replicating? Where is the repository of development knowledge? For a sophisticated sports culture like Australia's, we are totally unsophisticated in these matters. If we had any appreciation of the specific requirements of development coaching, our system would be all over this sort of information. The database would be bulging. We haven't developed anything like it.

There is no awareness of who has done a good job around the country. These coaches should be profiled, celebrated, harnessed. When you hear about the golden generation it's constantly with reference to the work done by Ron Smith at the AIS. Mark Viduka speaks a lot about his father and his club, the Melbourne Knights. Culture is obviously an important part of the development process and we've tried to nuke that too. We've got no appreciation of what we were good at, so we bomb everything. The NSL and many of its member clubs generated a fertile conversation about football but in our haste to become acceptable (to ourselves, to mainstream Australia via the A-League) we flushed that away. There's a measure of cynicism that accompanies this process because, with all the imported expertise, there comes a need to justify those coaching appointments. I've never heard any of the foreign coaches actually acknowledge that there was anything worthwhile that predated their arrival. It's as though they feel like – or worse, have been told – we are a useless flock who need shepherding to safety.

Previous achievements or successes are ignored. Rarely is any credit given. Either they don't care to ask or they are told not to bother. Or they might feel their role and remuneration would be compromised if they conceded that there is quality and knowledge residing in the game's history here. Our Aussie spirit is loved, they say. We're an athletic bunch who love our sport. Aussie players fight to the death. The subtext is that we're no good but we try hard. We accept that. We roll over and have our tummies tickled by it. It's reductionist and wrong and every new appointment proves the case; coming from countries where football is lingua franca, with financial resources and athletic talent that reflects that, the lesson is quickly learned that in Australia it's a fishes and loaves job, doing a lot with not much. They make no headway either and the easiest explanation is that Australia is a football wasteland.

If I were to coach another country's national team, I wouldn't know without asking and looking what was in the culture that drove them as people. I wouldn't walk in there blindly and make quick assessments, based on stereotypes. You can't succeed that way.

I'd been in the Australian game for eons, as an NSL coach and then as the national youth coach for seven years, and I was never asked by technical interlopers what I thought our core considerations should be regarding youth development. If I wasn't going to be asked, given my history, who was? My seven years were dismissed as an aberration. There can be no other explanation as to why that knowledge was just allowed to vanish. Although it didn't vanish, it stayed with me, and Australian football has been able to revisit that well. But there was no single-minded intent by the FFA, then or now, to plough that field with me.

The only thing I can see we've really developed is a keen instinct to tear something down and start again. That's the scorched earth reflex. Drastic renovation is required from time to time, no doubt, but after we've done the wrecking we don't then seem to be able to say where we're headed or what we're trying to achieve. For a close up look at a demolition and rebuild, you only have to look at Germany. After failure at Euro 2004 the DFB (German football's governing body) looked itself over in a full-length mirror. The decade-long rebuild now has its league flagship, the Bundesliga, firing on all fronts and the national team are champions of the world. Given the German penchant for engineering, I can't imagine for a second that they did the demolition without having first thought about what the rebuild was going to look like when it was done and how they were going to get there.

Instead of opening the door to more kids we're consolidating, which I take to mean treading water. But you can't tread water in professional sport. There are only two gears in sport, forward or backward, because if you stagnate, everyone around you is going to keep moving forward, and past you. Standing still is akin to death in this business. All our defeatist buttons are pressed and negativity goes into overdrive. It's such a counterproductive cycle. This is a very much a learned behaviour by Australian football communities, with deep roots through history. It's a destructive default position. There is no way that Australian football can realise its goals from the platform of a ten-team professional league. It is impossible to generate the volume of talent and games and opportunity from a footprint that small.

Football always waits for someone or something to validate it. We need a nationally coordinated approach that enshrines alignment across the various levels, harnessing a real belief in the game's future. I know the game has a big future. There can only be room at the game's top levels for people who see the size of its potential. And I mean really believe it, not just mouthing platitudes to snare a few corporate dollars here and there. I'm talking about setting the place alight in pursuit of what this game can be in Australia. That's a big vision for a big opportunity and there is a ridiculously big number of people in this country who will join us on that journey.

The fact that we are as competitive as we are, given how little we've put into the process so far, should embolden authorities to get stuck into this issue. Imagine how powerful we'd be internationally, via the A-League and the Socceroos, if these structural issues were dealt with. The failure to qualify for Rio 2016 puts the microscope on Australian football and youth development. That lens tells us everything about where the game is at and where we should go from here. Scorched earth on loop isn't the answer.

9

THE COACHING GENOME

There are many different descriptions of coaching and coaches, what makes them good, what makes them bad. People have different skill sets, different strengths and different weaknesses. Coaches work within those variables to manipulate the group in their charge into achieving an end, or ends. But while there are many variables among coaches, there are really only two types of coaches: those who work to get and then keep a job and those for whom coaching is about seeking new horizons.

The motivations for each are starkly different, even if on-field results might appear similar. I believe the more exciting type is the coach who looks to create something new or to take on special challenges. I believe that is the essence of the coach as an agent of change, the person who can enter an environment and make it better, for the long term. I am a coach who enjoys climbing mountains. I am a coach who must climb mountains. If I can set a lofty target and take a group – a team, a club, a national association – to a wonderful new place, somewhere not experienced or imagined before, to me that is what coaching is about. In realising that ambition, I know I will positively affect individuals and systems, all of which is good, although it's not my primary motivation.

From my earliest days, the pictures I had in my mind about what football is, what it should be and the things it should represent were set very firmly. In every job I have, I can't operate without bringing life to those images. That's what drives me and that's why, for me, coaching isn't about wins versus losses or keeping a job. Those things will look after themselves. My job, my aim and my essence, is to change things – perceptions, expectations, values, the status quo. Football teams are the tools of my trade.

People probably stop at this point and say, 'It's easy enough for the Socceroos coach to talk about stuff like this, he's at the top end of the pyramid.' My response would be that any success I have achieved is a result of this approach. I didn't battle through the previous twenty years of my career pragmatically accumulating enough wins to be credible. I am where I am because of the principles I embraced and the process I've undertaken from the very start. My success is the very beginning of the process, sustaining the process and the vindication of that process's outcomes. I try to tell people that whether it is coaching or something else, real success (the way I value it) only comes from a deep immersion in an adventure. That's what life should be to all of us. Of course I speak about football coaching specifically, but exactly the same principles apply to any walk of life, or any profession. You can work to get and keep a job or you can work to make something special.

My coaching mantra isn't some recently cobbled-together management speak, crafted for the public-speaking circuit. Too often observers focus on success and not the heart of the process that delivered that outcome. Glib analysis such as that disrespects what success is. Success isn't a facile construct and it shouldn't be represented as such. Success isn't about sprinkling a bit of magic dust over people to make them feel better. It can't be reduced to the power of positive thinking. To appreciate success you need to understand and embrace the depth of the processes involved. It is imperative for me to push people beyond the first line of the story or the results sheet. If success is really desired people have to take stock, decide what they want, focus, and climb that mountain. This, I think, is the basic truism confronting everyone. It just so happens that the thing that stirs me is football. I'm driven by the need to coordinate, cajole, sometimes coerce, a group of people to football specialness.

Irrespective of the type of coach, there is a raft of commonality in the details of the job. Different people are better or worse at handling those details. Coaching has changed from when I first began the senior journey at South Melbourne Hellas. Nowadays the person in charge does not have automatic authority. In my days as a player, walking into the first-team dressing room as a seventeen- or eighteen-year-old, I don't remember saying a thing for three years. That was the dynamic and hierarchy of the dressing room. If the coach had said, 'Ange, I want you to get your training gear on and run out of the rooms and straight off that jetty into the lake,' my response would have been, 'Okay, no problem.'

If I asked a player to do that today they'd ask why, did they have to, can they bring someone with them, what does the bottom of the lake look like, who's going to get them out when it's done? You need to be able to answer those questions, even if you're surprised they've come in the first place. But the key to all of it is making the player believe that jumping into the lake with his training kit on is a good thing, it has a purpose, he'll be better for it and so will the team. That can't be achieved if you just set him off saying, 'Do it.' It might have worked twenty years ago but it won't work today.

So if you're dealing with a group of people, and I deal with young men – even if they're thirty-two or thirty-three, they're all young men to me – I have to give them a compelling reason to do what I'm saying. To do this, two very basic things are fundamental that we sometimes take for granted when we talk about coaching.

The first is knowledge. Knowledge is paramount. Without it you can't answer questions. If a player approaches you and asks what to do in a certain scenario on the field, he needs to be sent away with a concise, definitive and correct answer to his question. It is impossible to provide that without the requisite knowledge in place. Bluffing your way through seven possible answers won't cut it. Crystal clarity is demanded. This isn't reserved only for on-field matters, although that's the key intersection for me when dealing with my players. The only way to develop and maintain that knowledge base is by being open, observing, talking, listening. I tell my players, 'If you meet someone interesting and you have only ten minutes with them, spend the first nine minutes listening. The key part of any conversation is the part where you listen.'

The second fundamental component to coaching is language, the method by which you impart knowledge to the group you're working with. We spend so much time communicating with our fingers nowadays, via text message or email or social media, that I feel the ability to deliver a message in person is being lost. At the most basic level, we're practising the more traditional form of communicating less, so people don't improve at it. Convenient but impersonal electronic messaging is dulling the dynamism of person-to-person contact.

One thing that really stimulates me in football is the need for good, sharp communication. Facebook or Instagram or text messages are completely useless in my line of work. When I need to get a message across, during a half-time break for instance, in real terms I have about three and a half to four minutes to make an impact. Sorting out problems in that condensed half-time period sorts the good communicators from the bad. Forget whatever you may presume about the coach having an impact when the game is going on. They can't. As a player I heard coaches screaming at me from the sidelines, but had no idea what they were saying. There's just too much going on. Even when I scream from the sidelines now, which does happen, I sometimes think to myself, *What the hell am I doing, they're not listening.* It's usually got more to do with me relieving emotion than actually sharing information.

So the impact I have is condensed into a three- to four-minute span at half time. By the time I get to the dressing rooms, forty-five minutes of football are spinning around in my head. Things my team has done and that the opponents have done. The game's frantic, the crowd's going off and there might have been a refereeing controversy that's caused a stir. Players are filing into the dressing room in various states of ease or unease. Emotion is usually high and they need to settle. Assistant coaches are loading me up with the ideas they have and the observations they've made. The medical staff are updating me on this or that player. There are myriad moments from the game flying through my memory. Amid the maelstrom, as a coach I have to pick out the two most important things that need to be said to players who are sitting and waiting for guidance. I have about ten to fifteen sentences to do it in. If you bugger up any of those sentences, can't find the words, mix the message, stumble, or can't see clearly what you have to tell these guys, those precious three minutes are whittled down to two minutes, to one minute. Meanwhile, you're potentially losing the players. Maybe they're becoming more confused or angry or empty, or all three. Then the referee knocks on the door and instructs the players to retake the field. As a coach I have to get that moment right and I can't do it by posting a message on Facebook or sending an email to the entire office. This isn't the only place where a coach works, of course, but those are the crucible moments.

One such moment was in the final of the 2015 Asian Cup. From the first preparation camp I'd been making a point about the book of Australia's football history, and the chapter it would include on the 2015 Asian Cup. I said to the players that they were the ones writing that chapter. This was the ongoing theme, in the lead-up but certainly through the tournament itself. And D-Day for all this was at the end of ninety minutes in the tournament's final against South Korea.

We'd been leading the game one–nil, care of Massimo Luongo's first-half goal. We were getting agonisingly close to winning the game inside the ninety minutes, until the star of the South Korean team, Tottenham Hotspur player Son Heung-min, scored a late equaliser. The Iranian referee, Alireza Faghani, blew for full time shortly after. South Korea had escaped defeat. Australia, my team, had squandered victory. There would be a very short break before the referee would start the thirty minutes of extra time.

Throughout the month of January I had reinforced with the players that they had the power to determine the historical record of this tournament. It was in their hands, or at their feet as it were. I knew that the players had prepared meticulously, they were fitter and stronger than their opponents. We'd worked extremely hard on achieving that. We also believed we were mentally stronger, which was the point of scheduling all those away friendlies after the World Cup. Six months on the road, no home games, we were aiming purely at toughening-up and battle-hardening the squad for moments like these. When the games were coming thick and fast during the tournament my guys were getting tougher and tougher with each game. Their belief and commitment grew commensurate with their desire and determination.

There was constant feedback from our sports science boss, Dr Craig Duncan, who was filling them up with information and data, showing them how strong they were; stronger than any other team, particularly at the back-end of games. He wasn't whispering aspirational nothingness into their ears, he was showing them cold, hard numbers proving their performance and output. Assistant coaches Ante Milicic and Peter Cklamovski were pumping information to me and the players that our front-third actions (attacks) were more frequent than those of any other team. Both of them were obsessive in their relaying of information. There was no way any player could believe anything other than that we were the fittest, strongest and best. This was a repetitive, force-fed diet of encouragement and positive thinking that was based on data, not whim. Our game was built on grinding down our opponents and all the data was supporting the aim. There wasn't a player who didn't know the state of play.

So when the game reached its ninety-first minute, in stoppage time not extra time, the trophy was sitting pitch-side ready for presentation and we, on the bench, were all standing there right next to it, in nervous anticipation, waiting to be champions, there's hardly any time left on the clock. Then Son equalised for South Korea. Everything disappeared. All the build-up and talk and preparation, never mind ninety minutes of hard graft, destroyed in one moment by the master Korean. I had to make sure that this wasn't the feeling going into extra time.

It felt like the whole stadium had the air sucked out of it. You've never heard 80 000 people go from making a massive din to almost total silence so quickly. I understood what my players were probably feeling and knew they were going to need a jolt. I looked behind me and all the staff had just slumped in their chairs. They couldn't believe what had just happened. I couldn't either, but it wasn't for me to sit there with them and acknowledge the despair. I was reeling as well, to be honest. My head was spinning. But I had to compose myself because the players were walking over and I'd have to find the right words and assume the right body language. So I walked off on my own. This was going to be a critical message, I'd only really have seconds to deliver it and it had to be right. I needed space to formulate my message but also to create room to deliver that message. It would have been a mistake to make myself part of the atmosphere of the group as well as trying to say the key thing(s) to maximum effect.

As I'd meandered away from our guys I looked over at the South Korean team and they'd already slumped to the ground. The players were getting massages and taking in as much fluid as possible. I saw them, pretty spent, and realised my opportunity. I turned to my boys, having not seen what they were doing, but hoping to hell they were standing up. When I turned around I saw them all, every single one, standing up. The trainers were trying to give them water but a lot of the players, in an amazing sign of resilience, were shooing the help away. They were standing, tall and strong, just as all the analysis and data had suggested they would be, waiting for me to deliver my message. I knew what I was going to say but there would only be thirty seconds to say it. My choice was staying among the group and working around the individuals, hoping to get to each of them with something, or to hit them all at once with the pile driver.

The full stadium was just a backdrop now. We were

impervious to the atmosphere and anxiety. The focus of the team was centred purely on me, and my focus was purely on the lines I would deliver to push them to victory. I pointed to the Koreans.

'Look. They're on the ground. Everything we've spoken about for six months since the World Cup has led to this moment. We're stronger, we're fitter. Craig's been telling you and now you can see it for yourselves. We have more belief than they do because we know what we set out for. That hasn't changed one bit and it's now very close to happening. You've worked every minute of the last thirty days for this moment and you're ready for it. You will win.' And then, before they left, I said, 'And you'll make that chapter on the Asian Cup even more memorable.' With that I turned on my heels and went back to my seat. The players retook the field and made that Asian Cup chapter completely unforgettable.

If I hadn't been able to articulate that in the available thirty seconds, who knows what would have happened. If there'd been no talk about the writing history, if we hadn't been driven by that narrative throughout, my last comment would have been a very random one. But as it was, it wove into the story that had been at the forefront of everyone's six-month-long journey. If we hadn't made it very clear, from the outset, that winning the Asian Cup on Australian soil was the summit we were going to reach, I doubt the players would have been able to access the reserves necessary. If I hadn't played out that narrative in my own head a hundred times before I might have missed the opportunity to refocus our blokes, who had been so close to the ultimate success only to have it taken away late.

When two substitutes (Tomi Juric and James Troisi) combined to make the winning goal, on the back of a whole month of me repeating how important everyone in the squad was, even those players who didn't start games or play much, I knew all the messaging had been internalised. I saw Jason Davidson, the left back, still ploughing forward in extra time when he was exhausted and might have decided to save energy or to play it safe. Except that he'd been inculcated with 'go forward' and so was able to resist his fatigue and bomb-on at every cue.

We'd talked about trying to score every time we went forward, no matter who was playing or at what period of the game. Seeing all those dynamics come together, with players fatigued and playing under the enormous pressure of the Asian Cup final, that's what coaching is all about for me. Not just in that game but as the culmination of the entire journey. And the information I was giving the players, the encouragement, was all based on fact. The only thing that remained was the message, which at the very end was quite literally the same as it was at the very beginning; we're going to write the chapter on the Asian Cup and it's going to be a beauty.

People have said they thought that winning the Asian Cup was lucky. So too the seven grand finals I've been involved in either as player or coach, all victorious. Luck. Winning the first grand final with Brisbane from two–nil down with four minutes of extra time left, that was luck. The grand final win versus Perth and the Besart Berisha penalty, luck. At South Melbourne, when we were down two–one and won three–two, with substitute John Anastasiadis scoring with his first touch, luck. Of course it's not luck. These successes came on the back of a process. Luck isn't a defining factor at all. I'm not in the lottery business. Rolling the dice isn't in my DNA. Manipulating environments is.

Before the Asian Cup I made all the Socceroos stand up before the group and tell their story. It was not an easy exercise for them because, despite the fact that they are with each other twenty-four seven for an entire month, one mustn't assume that they ever have real conversations. Seated in a room, we went round one-by-one and the first couple of guys stood up and talked about being an international footballer and wanting to play for their country to make people proud, that sort of thing. Of course it's difficult to go first in a scenario like that but as we went around the group a couple of the guys began to open up a little more. They told stories about a mum or a dad who didn't have much but took them to training all the time. On the way home there'd only be five dollars to get something to eat and it didn't register with them at the time but the mum or dad wasn't eating because there was only enough money for one. So when they played that first game for the Socceroos they made sure that person got their shirt, to show the appreciation of the effort and support. Soon the whole room was buzzing. Some guys were getting quite emotional.

One of the most remarkable stories was told by Mark Bresciano. He had recently run into Alen Stajcic, who's now the coach of the women's national team, the Matildas. Alen told him that he'd been in the stadium for Australia's fateful play-off second-leg against Uruguay in 2005. In that game Mark scored the only goal in regular time, tying the game on aggregate and putting Australia within touching distance of our first World Cup in over thirty years. Alen told Mark that when he scored, everyone in the stands erupted. Yelling, waving scarves, throwing things, the whole lot. Except for one bloke in front of Alen, who had his head in his hands. When Alen tapped him on the shoulder he saw that the man was crying. He asked him if he was a

Uruguay fan, thinking he'd just been sat in the wrong section, but the man said, 'No, I'm Mark's father.'

Mark hadn't known about that until Alen told him, years later; he'd never seen his father cry. But that story crystallised for him the significance of playing for the Socceroos, what it meant to his family and the people in his life.

With the ice broken, the first speakers asked to go again so they could say more and feel part of what was happening. I realised two things during that exercise. First, people don't talk much any more, and second, there's immense power in language and storytelling. The group was very different when they left that room.

By declaring their allegiance and making themselves vulnerable, the players created empathy. Knowing why and how each came to be in the room made the kinship stronger. The players who didn't start games or play as much as others didn't feel ostracised. People felt informed, involved and valued. All the while I was reinforcing the idea that for the Asian Cup project to work we were going to need everyone, in some capacity, at some stage. Everyone felt covered and supported, no one was exposed or isolated. There were forty sets of hands writing the story.

I didn't use the same approach prior to the World Cup in Brazil. The lead-up to the tournament was so ridiculously short and, with so much to do, I felt I was making things too overwhelming for this new team. For the World Cup I needed every waking moment just to instil confidence in the team, to get more and more belief into them so that we could reach the necessary competitive level.

Contrary to the Asian Cup preparation I didn't actually want them to invest too much of themselves personally or emotionally. The Brazil adventure came too early in proceedings and I really didn't know which players would be long-term prospects. I didn't want to load them up because, if things didn't work out, I didn't want them to unravel. I needed them to go out onto the field knowing that I had their back and they were to do their best irrespective of what happened. There wouldn't be any negative repercussions and every experience would be a positive outcome for us. If anything turned sour, I would take total responsibility. I would carry that burden. I didn't want them overwhelmed by the feeling that their country and their families were depending on them. That is sort of implied anyway and I didn't want to exacerbate the pressure. We would develop into that, after the World Cup and in the build-up to the Asian Cup. That's the reason that team meeting before the Asian Cup was such a powerful one. The players had been through a lot together but, up until the Asian Cup, they hadn't actually really known much about one another.

I knew that if the World Cup didn't go well, we had enough time to build them up. But the fact is the bedrock of belief was laid down in Brazil. I kept saying to the players that anything we faced afterwards would be easier than playing defending champions Spain in a World Cup game. Nothing is going to be as hard as playing Holland after they've just beaten Spain. Nothing is going to be as hard as playing Chile, the most difficult team to play at the World Cup, in the opening game, with the whole world watching and with us so inexperienced. The players got through all of that impressively. That was part of climbing the summit. Had I been a coach content with circling base camp – a coach who works only to keep his job – I may well have opted for 'experienced' players and not exposed younger players to that level of competition. A lot of commentary would have supported that, by the way. I wasn't going to do it that way though. Climbing the summit was my aim; the Asian Cup summit, that is. This is a clear example of the difference between the two types of coaches as I see them. At times there was a barrage of dissension along the way, but it didn't bother me because my focus was beyond all of it. Unless a course is set out, a course to challenge and change, a coach is vulnerable to the insatiable beast of winning this week, losing the next, or whatever it may be. Win to stay in the job for another week. Lose this week and start worrying. It's no way to achieve anything and I wasn't going to run the Socceroos program along those lines.

Most successful coaches are driven by the same paradigm. Pep Guardiola and José Mourinho have teams that play differently, but they are driven to ascend mountains. Mourinho wants to win, in as many different leagues as possible and with different teams. To win the English Premier League with two different teams – unprecedented – that'd be the sort of thing that drives him. Drives what players he recruits, the processes he implements, the stories he tells, the group energy he activates. Guardiola is hell-bent on winning too, but with a style that nobody else can match or master. For neither man is it about keeping a job, or evading pressure or criticism or scrutiny. They're not seeking a position of comfort, away from haranguing media or viperous fan sentiment. That place can't exist for them, given what they set out to do. If they wanted that 'safe' place they wouldn't do what they do – or find success.

I often give this message to coaches when I speak with them at conferences or elsewhere. I get a mix of responses. Some people get enlivened by it and some are intimidated. I can see people rifling through their own profile, trying to work out which type of coach they are. Some can't work it out. Many have never even thought about anything like this before. Coaching has been just part of their progression.

Ultimately the onus is actually on the employers of the coaches, rather than the coaches themselves. An organisation has the responsibility of understanding what they need and want for their set-up, and ensuring they get someone with the appropriate mentality. The people appointing the coach need to know where they are heading. There have been plenty of clubs without any framework, direction, ambition or image of what they want to be, and then they appoint a coach who's never thought of what type of coach he or she wants to be. What a woeful combination. Talk about a pointless, loveless marriage. No wonder the coach–club divorce rate is so high.

There's no point in an organisation espousing summit-climbing ideals and then appointing coaches with their eye on base camp. It's so easy on a PowerPoint presentation for a club to say this or that about themselves only to fail with their key appointment because they don't understand what and who a coach is. Often they can't decide if they want (or are unable to recognise) a coach who is going to embrace the challenge and grow the business or a coach who is going to be worried about keeping his job.

Rookie coaches might feel as though they don't have much of a choice in the role they take on. They feel they just need to get going and that's probably reasonable. I was in a similar position when South gave me the job as a thirty-year-old. I had no experience at that level. But coaching had been my focus since I was a kid and that made a difference to how I started my career, the choices I made and what I placed emphasis on.

Having said that, five games into my debut season we were last in the league. It was a Sunday and our game was the last of the weekend. I was sitting watching the *On the Ball* program on SBS. The NSL table came up on screen. South Melbourne, last. The phone rang. It was Raul Blanco, a former NSL coach, the Sydney 2000 Olyroos coach and a coach in the national team set-up. We talked for a short while but the crux of Raul's message was, *Listen, I know it's a tough time, but stick at it.*

I thought it was a nice call for him to make. It hadn't actually registered with me that perhaps my job was on the line. The South thing could have collapsed that Sunday afternoon and I hadn't even thought about it until Raul called. Perhaps he'd heard something, or his experience told him trouble wasn't far away. Anyway, we played our game against Newcastle, Ivan Kelic scored a jammy goal and we won one–nil. It was a turning point, everything started falling into place from then on.

I had never considered that I might be cut but I

guess Raul's experience was telling me that was possible. I'd felt the team was progressing even without winning and, anyway, it was very early in the season. But club officials can get nervous. They are often on a hair-trigger when it comes to coaches. If job security had been my driver that phone call from Raul may have turned me to jelly. We may or may not have won that afternoon, I may or may not have kept my job that day. But the point is that, if ladder position had been a fixation of mine, even with my history at Hellas, I wouldn't have been long for the job.

One of the great variables in coaching is player recruitment and retention. Mistakes can be made and, in an environment where every penny counts, the science of list management takes on an even greater significance. In some parts of the football world a recruiting mistake is corrected by signing a cheque to pay off the time remaining on a player's contract. Not so in Australia, where the A-League is cash-challenged and bound by salary cap restrictions. Paying out player contracts can't happen without salary cap implications. So as a coach you have to work through mistakes as best you can. It can be very challenging.

I've made it a practice to sign people before players. That is, character and personality are the primary considerations, above technical acuity. I have had to learn lessons along the way to get to that point. Even then, I don't always get it right. I have to find players with a philosophy and mentality that aligns with what's needed, rather than judging solely on their playing ability. When I've got it wrong it has usually been about personality and not the playing ability.

Marcos Flores is a good example of that. Marcos can play, certainly, but he was nowhere near in line with what I was trying to build at Melbourne Victory. The flipside to him is Besart Berisha. When I signed him at Brisbane, his playing ability and CV weren't anything that flash compared to other players being presented to me. But talking with him it became very clear what made him tick and what his values were. He's the type of guy who goes to war at training, never mind in games. I wanted that. He's proven himself to be a winner by securing championships with both Brisbane Roar and Melbourne Victory. He's a champion, a signing I definitely got right, and one that reaffirmed for me the need to get the person right before thinking about the player.

Given the difficulties of recruitment and retention, I refrain from investing personally in players. I've always tended to keep my distance and over time it's become even clearer that I need that distance to be effective. It enables me to make hard decisions, free of sentiment. There is no awkwardness and my conscience can remain clear. If someone's not fitting in then I have to find somewhere in the organisation where they can still feel a part of things without disrupting anything. If that can't be done then clearly I have to exclude that individual. It's sticky and tricky, but it's necessary.

Keeping my distance from players also serves to keep them guessing, keeps them on edge, which is very important. Plenty of players talk about it, it drives them nuts. For me it's turned out to be a very important management tool: standing quietly, observing and keeping talk to a minimum. Strange as it may seem, I'm actually a social animal and really enjoy people's company, it's just that this part of me gets little or no oxygen in the professional environment. After a while I assume that people can tell the difference between 'Coach Ange' and 'Relationship Ange' (if I can borrow that from *Seinfeld*) but that isn't always the case.

Recently I went to have a coffee and a former player of mine, Nick Ward, was running the café. He came over to Georgia and me. Our baby son Max was bouncing around on our laps. It was quite a convivial atmosphere. Nick came to serve us but he was really reserved. I had to tell him to relax. He looked at Georgia and said, 'I can't relax around this guy.' I was still someone who unnerved him. I wasn't his coach any more but his default position around me was to wonder what I was thinking. He couldn't turn that switch off.

But that approach keeps the playing field level for everyone and allows me to scrutinise them. Nobody knows what I'm going to do or say, nobody knows where they sit with me. I don't establish any hierarchy or habits because I change from day to day, or at least reserve the right to. Sometimes I won't even do anything and the players will feel I've shifted something, or that the mood's changed. Or they've created a shift themselves. If I see them going off track I'll pull things back into line, but I'm pretty happy to leave players to themselves. They get the drift pretty quickly. The point behind all of this to ensure that no player feels safe in their position, that no entitlement or incumbency exists. They need to adjust to that environment and work out what is required of them.

The reality is when you're climbing towards the summit you've got to keep people on edge, constantly. That's my job. Climbing a mountain can become dangerous anytime. Individuals can come a cropper, endangering themselves and the party. If you're not alert you'll slip on a ledge and, the closer to the summit, the more precarious the ledges. Allowing people to get comfortable leads to complacency, which can be fatal. I won't let people feel comfortable. People can feel comfortable when they retire or when they're playing for another coach. That's not going to happen with me. This is how I get the best out of people and that's how we achieve our goals. I run a tight ship on matters like this and there is no room for negotiation.

Perhaps my reputation preceded me when I started at the Socceroos. Soon after my announcement as coach, three or four players retired before I'd even had a chance to talk to them. My style is different from what they were used to and maybe at their stage of career they felt they deserved some certainty. I can understand why they walked away but providing certainty to any player is impossible for me. Irrespective of the player involved, it would be incompatible with everything I've done. My decisions are based on the form of players and the needs of my team. There are no other considerations. I had it in my mind that regeneration of the squad was required but, regardless of age, I wasn't going to exclude anyone who could contribute. Some experienced players decided they didn't want to have to reassert their credentials. I respect that choice. But I couldn't change the way the project had to be conducted to accommodate that.

Publicly there was a lot of support for those experienced national team players. Lots of people felt they deserved something, although short of a guaranteed place in the team I couldn't say what exactly that would have been. I was focused on the journey ahead but I did reflect on the departure of some of that generation's big names. I'm big on celebrating the game's history and its players, and there were some of our sport's heroes in that group. I didn't have any problems with the guys who'd made their own call, that was their decision and their timing. I did struggle with the Lucas Neill situation though.

Being the captain and leader of the country for such a long time, Lucas had had a celebrated career. Regrettably it finished on the end of a phone line. The end for Lucas shouldn't have been a call from me telling him he wasn't going to the 2014 World Cup. I wonder if he would have felt any better if I'd told him in person. Maybe I should have taken him out to dinner.

The way my own playing days ended hung over me when Lucas's career finished. I'd been with South Melbourne since I was nine years old. I was captain of the first team at twenty-two. We'd won two championships. At twenty-six years of age I played my last game, 11.30 a.m. on a Sunday at Middle Park, in an Under 20s game. I was limping around the field. Nobody had the gumption to say, 'Ange, that's it mate. You're done.'

They just let me wither away. And they did it because they genuinely felt sorry for me. I don't know if I would have felt any better if someone had sat me down earlier. However it happened, I still would have thought it a bitter ending. I'm very conscious of that with every player I've had to deal with on that subject. When the time has come, there is no point mucking around.

I had to do it with Micky Petersen, a former team mate of mine. He was a senior figure at Hellas, a superb player, and one of my great mates. How do you break the news to someone like that? He thought he could still play. We had to have a coffee and I put him straight. He now says that was the best thing that could have happened but it probably shocked him at the time. It was difficult for both of us. Denial about a career ending is a huge thing for many players. Delivering that final message is perhaps the most unpleasant part of my job.

I do wonder if, with Lucas Neill, there was another way. There may not have been, but I'm still dissatisfied by how it unfolded. His last appearance for the Socceroos was in Sydney in November 2013, in a friendly match against Costa Rica. Lucas was getting heckled by some fans. He reacted to the taunts. He felt he had to speak against them, against their lack of support, railing against the un-Australianness of it all. I felt he was carrying way too much of a burden. This was not about him. That was the point I'd wanted to make clear to him and everybody else when I took the job. This was about our country, not any individuals. Lucas shouldn't have presumed to carry a bigger burden than any other player. Coming into the job, I felt the

Socceroos had become more about individuals than the national team as a whole. That's not what playing for your country is about. I was looking to shift the dynamic.

When Lucas reacted to those fans I said to him the burden was mine to carry, not his. As coach that is my job. If things don't go well I have to answer the questions, the player's job is to play. I don't know if what I said had any impact on him. Ultimately, however, the equation was pretty straightforward; he was desperate to play at the World Cup but he hadn't played enough football in the lead up. Not even close. He was struggling to even get a club.

The decision to cut Lucas was the easy part. The logistics of communicating that decision to him were going to be more difficult. I remember having a chat with Frank Lowy and David Gallop about it. I said that I thought I needed to fly to the UK and sit down across the table from him, to tell him in person where things were at. It just didn't work out. Time was getting tighter and I just had to make that phone call. It still rankles.

As phone calls go, it was a strange one. The pleasantries didn't take long to complete and Lucas began presenting his case. He'd played in an Under 21s game and was getting stronger. He was trying to convince himself as much as me, I think. He said he'd had an issue with his hamstring but that was done with now and his progress had been very good.

I had to interject. 'Lucas, it's gone too far. I've got to make the call now. Because of who you are I think it's better I make the call early, rather than have it drag on and muddy the waters later on. Let's deal with it now. You're not coming to Brazil.' The phone went quiet before I heard, 'Okay.' I told him it was his news to handle how he wanted. He made it clear he wouldn't be saying anything. 'I'll go to ground. If you change your mind let me know because I'm playing in a game next week.'

I wasn't going to change my mind. I hadn't reached that point of the project without being very clear in my mind where Lucas was at. When I got off the phone I realised it was the first time I'd ended a story only to be told by the person on the other end that the story might have one more chapter. It was strange, but there was no equivocation on my part. The book was closed. I'm sure even after the phone call Lucas was thinking I'd see the error of my ways. I couldn't possibly be taking Alex Wilkinson or Bailey Wright to a World Cup instead of him, surely?

It's almost three years since that phone call and he hasn't surfaced, so he was true to his word. He seems to have gone into hiding and I sort of wish that wasn't so for one of our greatest-ever Socceroos.

It might have been more difficult to deal with Lucas's non-selection if I wasn't emotionally detached.

While the situation was difficult, I'd served a good apprenticeship with separating myself from players at South Melbourne. Particularly poignant were my dealings with Paul Trimboli. Trimmers was my best friend from my playing days. From the moment he arrived as a young seventeen-year-old, without a driver's licence, I swept him up under my wing (and into my car). We almost lived next door to each other too. But as soon as I became coach at Hellas I had to cut off from Trimmers. It was strange. After virtually living in each other's pockets, I didn't have any social contact with him for three and a half years. No contact at all, and he was the captain of the club. I was very sensitive to the possibility that people would look at our friendship and see favouritism, or that he got some sort of special treatment. I needed to be able to make decisions about him without any hesitation, if I felt the team needed it. Thankfully that very awkward circumstance never arose.

Trimmers being who he is, I never had to say anything. He just knew, he understood. He jokes about it now; I was a grumpy old bastard at the age of thirty. He laughs because he knew the other side of my character. But he was very driven as a player, and the captain as well, so he bought in and never let on or attempted to quell the angst among the players. 'Don't worry, he's not really like that.' He could have skewered my whole persona. But that would have also skewered the project we'd embarked on at the club, and his own dreams too. He was as focused as anyone on success. When I left South Melbourne we immediately picked up where we left off and started socialising again. He baptised my son Max.

I run the whole show like this. Staff, like players, must be on edge. I tell them enough so they're not working in the dark and can stay across their brief, but they have to keep alert. In relation to me and whether I think they're doing a good job, I just stay quiet. As with Nick Ward in his café, I've had former staff relay to me times when I've said 'well done' to an individual or a group and people have been cartwheeling and high-fiving.

I hear stories like that a lot and pretty much every time it surprises me. I guess I'm a bit disconnected from the impact I have around the place. I don't socialise with the people I work with, even if we're in camp and there's a night where they all go out for a dinner. I'll stay in the hotel, tucked away in my room. It's my personal style, not one that I would necessarily prescribe for anyone else. I need that distance to be able to make cold, logical decisions. If I falter in my decision-making because a relationship has blurred the line, I endanger the whole project.

When he was our team manager at Brisbane, Trimmers used to tell me this running joke that nobody wanted to sit next to me on interstate flights. It'd be like the booby prize. When the boarding passes were being distributed the players would jostle to make sure they weren't sitting next to me. Invariably that pleasure would fall the way of one of the hapless young guys, who just did what they were told. Their reward was to sit in stone silence next to me. They'd look straight ahead for the whole flight. The trip west to play Perth Glory always produced the biggest scramble in the departure lounge. I could see the staff, too, shuffling into position around Trimmers, who had the tickets, trying to avoid 'the seat'. It made me chuckle.

It is often difficult though. My personality isn't entirely compatible with how I set up my work environment. I'd love to kick back and have a beer with my colleagues. I hear the staff laughing and telling a story about something that happened at dinner while I was in my room watching re-runs of *M*A*S*H* or something. But that's the discipline required for success. One thing I know, I am very disciplined. I don't waver. I won't allow my players to waver either. I'm making my own sacrifices and asking them to make theirs. There can be no shortcuts.

Obviously there have been many individuals over my twenty-year coaching career who've piqued my interest, but I've just had to let the opportunity to interact pass by. There is no question that I have missed out on some really positive exchanges, both in a personal and professional sense. This became apparent again with Socceroo central defender Trent Sainsbury, during the victory lap following the Asian Cup win. He came up to me in his 'champions' tee shirt, wearing a ridiculous hat, backwards, and said to me, 'Boss, it's been emotional.' I'd never spoken with him. I don't know if he was winding me up or entirely sincere, opening up. Because of his manner, it seems to me that he's a bit of a throwback to the kaftan-wearing liberal crowd of the 1970s. Part of me was interested in engaging with him and chewing the fat but I had to turn, walk away and laugh to myself.

I didn't respond to Trent, I haven't to anyone before him when I found myself in similar scenarios, and I can't see myself doing anything like that from here on out. I'll leave each winning dressing room behind, refusing to indulge the urge to celebrate, because I don't know when I might have to make a tough call on someone in that room. That instinct to mix with the players is overridden almost immediately because I know there is still more to do, there is still a summit to reach. I can't afford to party on a narrow ledge because I might topple.

Every coach is different in this sense. I can only do

things the way I know works for me. I remember Trimmers, and others, talking about Englishman Terry Venables as the outstanding coach they had in their time with the Socceroos. He was a massive social beast, very personable and affable. If he saw a player walking through the foyer he'd call them over for a chat and a cup of tea. There's not an Aussie player I know who played under him who has a bad word to say. And his record is very good. Reputedly he put the game into a new light for the players, provided them with new clarity. Tough calls always have to be made though, even by gregarious coaches, and I don't really know how they do it. Sitting down for coffee one minute and cutting players the next. I have to keep distance so that my decisions remain unfettered.

Coaching isn't so much a job as a lifestyle choice. The thing about lifestyle choices is that problems aren't eliminated just because you're doing what you believe you're meant to be doing. However, ensuring that you stick to the core principles and meaning of the journey will pull you through the inevitable difficulties. This is true of my coaching career, during which there have been many challenges. The only thing that pulls me through to the other side of a problem is complete commitment to the story that was conceived in the first place. Indeed, the hurdles become part of what I'm doing, who I am. They fortify the journey. When you've identified a summit and your heart, soul and mind are consumed by reaching it, the problems that arise along the way will be cast aside. Those hanging around base camp can only ever imagine the real depth of that truth.

10

SUPERSTARS

To have marquee players or not to have marquee players – that is the question facing the A-League. Or at least it seems to be. Of course any league would endeavour to have the best and brightest players in their competition. However, when players are categorised as marquee or not, the discussion gets derailed.

The domestic competition is the lightning rod for the strengths and weaknesses of a country's football. All is laid bare; the things a country or culture celebrates as well as its hang-ups and foibles. The same is true of the A-League, where the issues and debates are symptoms of the bigger picture. The marquee player issue is but one example, and it rages as a topic of conversation.

Everybody in the game experienced the impact of Italian superstar Alessandro Del Piero when he signed for Sydney FC in 2012. The *Sydney Morning Herald* probably set the tone when it published the entire back page of the Saturday edition in Italian as a gesture of welcome and a statement on the significance of the player's arrival in Australia. Del Piero wasn't the first huge name to sign on, and hopefully he won't be the last, but he's certainly been the biggest so far. The impact he had on key measures, in particular attendance and viewership, has people hankering for similar investments and experiments. There can be no question that the names of famous players drive publicity and exposure. But big names come at a cost, so the question is how to finance the best possible players coming to our shores, as well as how to exploit their time here in the most effective way.

The overriding problem seems to be a belief in simple, singular solutions to football's challenges, when they don't exist. There is no silver bullet for anything in football, but 'marquee players' are peddled as the cure for everything. I think we've got the marquee concept wrong. For a start I'd do away with the term itself. I think it distracts, and detracts, from the main game, which should be to broaden the overall strength of the game in a coordinated way. A label such as 'marquee players' almost by definition encourages the belief that marquees will fix everything; if we don't have them we can't succeed and when we do have them we can all sit back and wait for the success that will be a matter of course. That's in addition to the problem of categorising players in that way, which causes an unjustified discrepancy of attitudes in the system.

The marquee concept was well entrenched in the NSL too, although without the same label. The procurement of high-profile players, principally from Europe, has been more or less ever-present in Australian club football for decades and the longitudinal analysis seems to suggest that the impact has been little more than blips and spikes along the way. That may be a harsh assessment, because I can easily accept the incremental effect those blips and spikes have over time. All such things contribute to the greater effort. However the inescapable truth is that, for all the energy and excitement and money that has repeatedly been devoted to marquee programs (whether thought of in those terms or not), we seem to repeatedly find ourselves back at the same point: what now, how do we grow the game's appeal, and who do we get to do it?

Thinking back to my childhood I remember that in the first season of the NSL, in 1977, famous players were well represented. Over forty years of watching football, there is one game from that year that is seared into my memory more than most others. My dad and I were regular attendees at Middle Park, South Melbourne's home ground. On this day Hellas were playing St George. Malcolm 'Supermac' Macdonald was South Melbourne's prize recruit, for St George it was Charlie George. The ground was packed, maybe 18 000 people. There was no room to move. Macdonald was a powerhouse centre forward with a hammer of a left foot, and a big name in top-flight English football at the time. Charlie George was in that first wave of football celebrities; he had a playboy lifestyle but he was a player who was amazing to watch. With his socks down around his ankles and his mullet dancing in the breeze, his feet would dance around would-be defenders. They were exhilarating players and the opportunity to see both at the same time had Middle Park splitting at the seams with eager fans. To add to the occasion, Supermac scored two for us that day. Unfortunately St George ended up victorious, three–two, courtesy of a Charlie George winner. It couldn't have panned out any better for the organisers. The ground was buzzing and in recollection my memory still does too. The impact on this young boy was immense.

Over the next thirty-odd years various NSL clubs dipped their oars into the water with big-name players. But the ultimate demise of the NSL showed that big-name foreigners alone weren't enough to save the competition. The problems around the NSL weren't going to be resolved through one mechanism. With a more coordinated approach, perhaps the big imports would have had a lasting impact on the competition itself, rather than just living on in the memory of kids. I would hope the marquee discussion in the A-League would heed the lessons learned in the NSL. The A-League and Sydney FC, post Del Piero, reinforce the point. Where's the legacy of that large investment?

Football in Australia has habitually failed to link the star factor with building the league's fundamentals, such as marketing, fan engagement, awareness and accessibility. By 2016, and with decades of commercialised and commodified sport now behind us, we should have a far more developed and sophisticated approach to these things. The NSL operated in a part-time, semi-professional sporting world and failing to connect their marquee players with broader growth was perhaps forgivable. Not so nowadays.

Notwithstanding this, the most important contribution of a big name is the impression they have on kids. To that end, it may be way too soon to understand the legacy of Del Piero at Sydney FC. (I use him as the example because he's the most recent and arguably the biggest name to play in the A-League.) If it's agreed that producing fans of the future is a key driver in marquee player recruitment then one would think there'd be a concerted effort to plan marquee player succession. I can't see that anything like that exists at all, which suggests the whole thing dangles in a strategy-free zone.

Football is skewed heavily towards a young demographic and it's reasonable to expect that young people will be even more attracted to football in the future. The game's participation numbers make it clear what a big opportunity that is. The growth of A-League fan bases over generations is something the league can't really test yet, given its own relative youth. We might not be able to measure Del Piero's impact on the A-League or Sydney FC's fan base for some years. But having completed eleven seasons, we are now starting to see kids who were once fans of A-League clubs becoming players for those clubs. We'll also begin to see second-generation fans of the A-League coming through, taking after their family. These are very important factors for a sport.

It's one thing to surmise, or decree, that the league needs marquee players and quite another to find the right guys to fit. Marquee names must play a big role in welding young people to the game and to clubs, so things need to be done astutely. It's great when it works but, in the eleven seasons completed so far, the real successes have been relatively few. After the immediate spike in interest, the feel-good factor dissipates pretty quickly. It is like a child building a sandcastle on the ocean's edge; so exciting when the water comes in and fills the moats and passageways, but it takes next to no time for the retreating water to take everything away again, leaving nothing behind other than a vague outline. Too often the marquee concept has been a sandcastle rather than something that develops strong foundations.

There are a lot of glib statements made on the topic, but targeting big-name players can be very difficult. For these types of players to be worth the investment, fans have to be able to relate to them. Spending seven-figure sums on European internationals who are completely unknown in Australia is almost a total waste of money. Very good players can be found for far less money. The evidence suggests that clubs do better with a $300 000 foreigner than a $1-million-plus European international who has no profile in Australia. When the 'lesser' players (again, the categorisation brings unjustified negative connotations) work out, surely it would make sense to market them and build their profile on the back of their good football. The game has failed pretty dismally on that front. I think of the likes of Thomas Broich and Besart Berisha, two players I brought to the competition. They cost a fraction of Del Piero, naturally. However their appeal is huge and most definitely undersold. This structural weakness in the league must be fixed.

———

At the time of writing, it seems Tim Cahill may join the A-League. For me, he would be the ultimate marquee player for our game right now. Whatever people think or say about him, the impact he would have as an A-League player would be stratospheric. He's a huge name with a huge CV, and people relate to him. He's one of ours, too, which you'd think is an advantage. And it's not as though he is approaching the end of the road and looking to be superannuated. Timmy is a commercial beast, for sure, but he's utterly committed to playing as well as he can for as long as he can. He remains focused on qualifying for the 2018 World Cup. Tim's presence would permeate every part of our society.

The marquee concept, in its purest sense, seeks to buy the brand and profile that come with a player's name, and equates that with a marketing plan. We sign the player and that is the marketing. At almost every turn we wait like lapdogs for every utterance from these 'great players', in the hope that good favour is bestowed upon our country and our league. 'Australians are really friendly' ticks the first box. 'I was surprised by the standard of the league' makes us feel vindicated. My major issue with the entire movement is that these are expensive exercises in seeking football validation. Apparently we still need someone from outside to make us feel worth anything. It's not that trying to get the best players is a bad thing, quite the contrary. If big-name acquisitions are patched around a more robust sense of self then we can really start cooking with gas. For me the biggest goal we can score is to deal with the internal unease, which affects pretty much every part of our sport. Inadvertently, the current marquee strategy exacerbates rather than remedies that.

Self-image is the axis around which all these themes rotate. It's impossible not to arrive at that point when you consider how little emphasis has been put on promoting the very good 'non-marquee' players in the league. The whole thing reflects a gross laziness, neglect or ignorance in marketing or at the administrative level. Believe it or not, a figure was quoted in the press, which I've heard verified since, that one capital city A-League club had a marketing budget of $25 000 for the season. In 2016, we can't delude ourselves we're making progress with pitiful amounts like that. Marquee players can't fix that malaise. At best they can paper over the cracks.

It would be wrong to give the impression that I don't support recruiting star players. The opposite is really the case. There's no doubt the league got a huge boost out of Del Piero, and other players, being here. Sydney FC certainly did, their crowds and membership and international exposure all increased. And what's often forgotten is that Del Piero came into a pretty ordinary team that was struggling. If Sydney had won the competition, that might have made him seem more affordable. They would then have played in the Asian Champions League on top of it all, and maybe the returns there would have been significant. Perhaps it was just a timing thing and the parameters were wrong.

There were stories circulating that Del Piero was difficult to manage. His expectations were fairly demanding. There was a separate dressing room for him and the story went that he kept himself at some sort of distance from the team. These things have to be dealt with on an individual basis, and it's hard to pre-scribe a management strategy from afar, but I know I would have dealt with it. I can't say if he would have done the same thing with me but that's what man man-agement is, dealing with these things as they come up and, importantly, finding out as much as you can before a deal is done and the player is brought in.

People kept telling me that Tim Cahill was going to be a handful, but there's not been an ounce of concern. He has totally bought into the team ethos. There was one incident that nobody outside the team would have noticed but shows exactly how Tim stands with the team. In the World Cup qualifier against Bangladesh in Perth, I left Tim on the bench. I told him I wanted to start a couple of the younger guys, but I'd been engaging with him the whole time. I put him on the field with about fifteen minutes to go. Mark Milligan, the captain for that game, made his way to Tim to give him the captain's armband, a respectful gesture. Tim didn't take the armband, telling him 'No Millsy, you're the captain. I'm fine.' This is the guy people were telling me was self-absorbed, who thought it was all about him, all that kind of stuff. But at that moment his commitment was entirely to the team. Seeing that, I knew what space I had him in. Maybe Del Piero wasn't prepared to compromise and adapt to the environment in which he'd found himself and that's why he kept his distance. I can only speculate.

At Melbourne Victory I wanted a high-profile player. I wanted to meet that expectation because Victory is a big club and that is what big clubs do, manage big personalities. People say Victory is very successful without the big names, which is valid. I was after Giorgos Karagounis, a Greek international who I thought would have made a huge impact, both via his profile and his playing qualities. Maybe Karagounis could have launched Victory to even greater heights. Boards talk in numbers and balance sheets, and they get nervous when the conversation inevitably turns to salary. I said to the guys at Victory that I'd never seen a balance sheet do a lap of honour on grand final day.

I'd imagined Karagounis being part of that lap.

I remember when Hungarian legend Ferenc Puskás was our coach at South Melbourne. His name gave us enormous credibility. FIFA's award for the most beautiful goal of the year is named after him, which gives you some idea. We'd go interstate and at the airport people would be thrusting babies into his arms for photographs. We knew there was something special about him and that made the rest of us feel good. It also elevated the club. The right person can have that impact. Put Del Piero into a Sydney team that was flying – who knows what it could have been.

Del Piero and the like are at one end of the spectrum, but one of the big holes in our system is the failure to make heroes of other guys we have here. Thomas Broich is the outstanding candidate in this category. He really shouldn't be able to walk down a Brisbane street without people knowing who he is. It certainly isn't his playing ability or his performances that stop that from happening. No reasonable and fair-minded judge could fail to be excited by his contributions. He's been amazing for his club, Brisbane, and the league itself. Three championships, two Johnny Warren Medals for best player in the competition, he's given absolutely everything. But he's a very well-kept secret. Thomas would be fine with the publicity, it's not as though he's shunned it, but neither does he chase the spotlight.

Imagine, over the five years he's been here, just spending a couple of hundred thousand dollars on marketing him. The profile of the player, club and league would be a mile ahead of where they are now. This is the guy who for years was followed by a German television company, compiling a documentary, because they thought he was going to be the next big thing in German football. The very same country that won the 2014 World Cup. Thomas had been earmarked for the playmaking role in that cohort of German players. For him one thing led to another and he ended up in Brisbane, where he's won everything. The Bundesliga's loss should have been our marketing and PR gain. There's been barely a ripple. We've successfully hidden his light under a bushel.

Thomas left Germany because of the fishbowl existence top-flight footballers have there, so maybe a huge publicity campaign would have been counterproductive. But compared to what he was used to anything we'd have done here would have been no problem. He's such an interesting guy. There are so many angles that could be taken. He's not the typical meathead from other sports, taking drugs or beating people up in nightclubs. He's a bit of a different cat, Thomas. He takes his guitar with him on away trips. He likes classical music and reads literature. But watch him play football on the weekend. He never misses a game. He is routinely the most fouled player in the competition and he never flinches. His consistency and quality are amazing. How is that not sellable?

Melbourne City's Bruno Fornaroli is another one. He could be the best player we've ever had here, so why are we waiting to pump him up? What more is it going to take to convince us he'd be worth that effort? It can't be right that we need someone else to value him before we appreciate and celebrate him, that we'll only be convinced he's something special if a club like Juventus want him. We have to believe in what we see every week, before our very eyes, and not be afraid to say so because we think we're sticking our neck out to be ridiculed.

At one point I made a comment that I thought Aaron Mooy was the best player in the competition and I was quizzed about whether I should be saying something like that. Seriously. That's what I saw, so that's what I said. I like watching him play, aside from being the national coach. He's an exciting player. My comments elevated his status, which in turn puts a bit of pressure on him. That's a good thing. We need to see how our players deal with that scrutiny and expectation.

I watch a minimum of twenty games of football a week, from around the world, looking at Aussie players. In terms of quality, the A-League games are consistently in the top few games I watch. I get a weekly global comparison, and I'm happy with where the league sits, particularly as a function of the resources that go into it. I feel comfortable saying that Aaron Mooy is Australia's best midfielder at the moment, or has been and can be. It's not a ridiculous statement. There are way too many people who don't say anything about the A-League for fear of being called ridiculous. The only ridiculous thing is that Bruno Fornaroli and Besart Berisha aren't all over the billboards of Melbourne.

I am supremely confident that the Australian product compares favourably. I come to this view on the back of the amount of football I watch and the detail by which I measure it. But we've also all seen it first-hand, at the Brazil World Cup, if we'd cared to really look. We're too happy to explain those performances away. You know the football product is good when you see Matty McKay, for example, Australian made to his bootlaces, in a World Cup Finals match standing toe-to-toe with Spain's midfield – the best of the generation – in a tired, inexperienced and beaten Australian team, still playing the ball as though he was in Spain's team. He, and others, passed that international test, yet people still question us. To ignore or deny what those guys achieved is more reflective of ignorance, cultural cringe or snobbery. I know I'm not making my memory up. I was there, pitchside in Brazil, with full knowledge of what our guys were up against, and I saw them confront that enormous footballing challenge. They measured up.

But we still found a way to not celebrate. We were still hesitant to glorify their performance. Of course failing to win fuelled that, but my thing wasn't the results. It was the way in which the guys played, it was courageous and exciting. It was there for everyone to see. I don't think the players got the credit they deserved. They pushed themselves to the limit and totally put themselves out on a limb to show their countrymen that they could match it with the very best in the world. As far as I'm concerned they achieved that. I'm as dirty as anyone that we didn't pick up any competition points. I know we should have got something out of both the Chile and Holland games. But really, the focus should have been on how these guys played in the face of that opposition. Instead, they remain largely unrecognised.

This lack of recognition, and other experiences, reinforces my belief that outsiders appreciate our football quality more than we do. I know that my insights and experiences are in constant demand from AFL and NRL clubs. Whether it's coaching, leadership, or whatever, my diary would be entirely filled if I accepted every approach. And for good money too. Football doesn't seek me out nearly so readily. Strange, I think, given I'm entrusted with Australia's national team. But apart from that, my experience and success isn't a well from which football seeks to draw. I wonder how football would have heralded Guus Hiddink if he had won the Asian Cup?

My twenty years of success in Australia hasn't yielded a great deal of interest from people inside the game. Is it because I didn't have a European playing career and so therefore can't have any real insight? The late Johnny Warren is the outstanding exception of a respected homegrown treasure, although in truth it was only after he passed away that he was really embraced as the visionary he was. If he was still alive I wonder if he'd be celebrated or just seen as the crazy, bitter old guy mumbling that our focus should be on winning the World Cup, not just making it. He made that statement in life and people hid in the shadows, but in his death people have been empowered by it.

When I went to South Korea I was greeted by a massive 40-foot banner, hanging in public, of their national coach Uli Stielike. And they finished second in the Asian Cup. I do wonder why it's so hard for Australia to pay homage, or celebrate the success of their team. In Australia after winning the Asian Cup there was nothing for us. Massimo Luongo was named player of the tournament and we slid into the back of our chairs and hoped no one would notice. It's like we were embarrassed, by Asia, by ourselves. Or by the wog son of the Greek migrant who coaches the team – you know, the type who has forever been a blight on the game in this country, who never played any real football himself anyway. I battle with this stuff not because of ego but because of disenchantment with the game. Our game didn't demand recognition for the Asian Cup and, disgracefully, the nation obliged.

Perhaps it was the same for Tony Popovic and the Western Sydney Wanderers when they won the Asian Champions League in 2014. That was a truly remarkable achievement. Talk about climbing Everest. But he and the club got no acknowledgement outside of their fans and people following the A-League. By the time we'd won the Asian Cup, we were the first-ever country to simultaneously hold the Asian club and national team titles. There wasn't a peep about this.

This is relevant to the marquee argument because if we're not going to celebrate a team winning the Asian Cup, on home soil, in the Asian Century, with an Australian coach whose twenty-year career has been successful, we're hardly likely to celebrate Archie Thompson or Thomas Broich or any of the other guys playing domestically. We'll only get excited about Del Piero or someone of that ilk. We need that to validate us. That's what marquees have been reduced to, it seems to me. Like the House of Windsor dropping by for a quick royal visit; we feel lucky that they've deigned to come here in the first place.

My personal validation comes from deeper within,

I don't measure myself by others' expectations. People wonder what the big-time opposing coaches say to me, if they congratulate me or whatever. What did Louis van Gaal (Holland), Vicente del Bosque (Spain), Jorge Sampaoli (Chile), Joachim Löw (Germany) or Uli Stielike (South Korea) say to me after our games? Were they complimentary? Did they pump me up? I couldn't care, not a jot. I don't need that. Van Gaal wasn't happy after our game, that's what I liked. I didn't need him to pat me on the back because we both knew what my team did to his. He didn't want to shake my hand. I thought that was brilliant. After the Chile game in Cuiabá I loved the look of relief on Sampaoli's face and his desire to get away. He was relieved because that third goal meant he wasn't going to have to face a rabid Chilean press, although we both knew that final goal masked how close the encounter in the Pantanal had truly been.

I couldn't be less interested in post-game platitudes from opposing coaches. I want to see them squirm during the game, that's my measure. When my team is giving it to their team and they weren't expecting it. I don't want to hear we play nice football. I'm not interested in patronising pats on the back. I want them angry. I want them pissed off and not wanting to play us any more. That's what I'm looking for in their coach's box. That tells me we're on the right path. When they fear us we know we're progressing. I don't need people telling me I'm a good coach, I already know that. I know my teams play good football. I heard Joachim Löw in the Germany dressing rooms at half time in our game. He was going off after we'd taken the game to them. That's what I wanted to hear. That's all I needed to hear.

People get vicarious validation hearing other people speak about me or the Socceroos. I don't need that, even if they do. I know the path we're on and what we have to do to reach our goals. I don't need to check that other people approve of us or respect us. They'll rate us because we're going to frighten the life out of them. Seeking validation from others is like chasing the wind. The only thing we chase is the ball and, by extension, excellence. Joachim Löw's opinion of my team doesn't impact on me at all, although I know favourable comments make others go weak at the knees. That's looking for the wrong thing. Worrying about the views of others, however eminent those people may be, is a distraction that only reduces effectiveness. Back yourself, back your competition, back your players and back your own ability. It will stand the test.

Australia should be beyond the need for ego stroking. We've qualified for consecutive World Cup finals. We sacked a coach after qualifying for the last one and that tells me more than anything else that we're ready to go to the next level. That was a gutsy and bold decision by Frank Lowy and David Gallop. For so long all we craved was qualification. Now qualifying for the World Cup isn't good enough by itself. That attitude is a step forward. That's the environment and ambition I want to feed and by which I want to be fed. Now I know it's serious. That single act told me there was a shift in the way we want to be perceived globally and domestically. I'll have a piece of that. I'm ready to put my shoulder to that wheel.

We do have these strong, really impressive moments, so I don't get why we cower at the sight of other challenges. I remember going into Frank Lowy's office before the Asian Cup. We were in the middle of a disastrous run at the time.

Lowy said, 'Ange, just tell me, how are we going to do [in the Asian Cup]?'

I told him that we'd be fine and that we were going to win it.

'No, don't tell me what you're going to tell the press, I want you to actually tell me what's going to happen. I want to know.' He wanted security and to know that we weren't going to be embarrassed.

'We're going to win the Asian Cup,' I said again.

'So you're telling me we'll make the final at least?' He couldn't let it rest. 'We've got to make the final.'

I repeated what I said the first time. I wasn't bluffing,

it's what I believed, so I said it and I kept on saying it. Of course that didn't guarantee me anything, but without saying it and believing it deeply I wouldn't have even made it to the first step. Your imagined outcome has to also be your opening gambit. Working things out along the way, seeing how things go, 'it depends' – that's too wishy-washy for me. We set the target and we let everyone know what it was. Of course that's sticking your neck out. If you don't hit the mark there's a queue of people ready to take to you with baseball bats. But that's no reason to avoid what must be done from the outset. Real success is only enjoyed as a result of the entire journey, including the very first steps and predictions. I don't think we could have won the Asian Cup unless we believed it could happen and were prepared to say so from the outset, being very clear about our ambition.

That's my type of marquee attitude. Not just some sort of parasitic program that seeks to suck the life out of a great player whose career is almost done. Marqueeism must be about attitudes, programs and leadership; a total conviction that the game is already massive and has even greater potential. That belief must be unshakable and the energy to enact it has to be unbounded by doubt. Tinkering around the edges won't be enough, that will only perpetuate the shortcomings. Don't be scared, be bold. People will follow an exciting and aggressive program.

That's the mandate. The top end has to catch up with the massive growth underneath it, not wait for the reverse. Our mentality of consolidation is wrong because it believes the A-League is ahead of the curve and we need to sit and wait for the base to catch up. The reality is the total opposite. The A-League is behind the game's growth curve, it should be busting its gut to be proactive and bold and to bridge that gap, to build a competition with a reach that absorbs the game's astronomical popularity.

Because when I stood up in front of the Socceroos after losing to Japan in Tokyo, just months before the Asian Cup, I couldn't equivocate when I said to the players that we'd win the tournament. I had to believe it and I did believe it. I wasn't thinking anything else. That's my job and if I'm not prepared to stick my neck out I may as well be replaced. I had to believe in the image I saw of Mile holding the trophy aloft in a blizzard of confetti. I had to project that image to the people in my orbit and they too had to be able to taste it, feel it and see it. Or else there is no point. I can't conceive of winning without that process. I've never won without it. And I believe if it's good enough for a national football team in an international tournament, then it's good enough as a guiding principle for the game at large.

In Tokyo, when I was pronouncing and declaring a future where we won the Asian Cup, we were in a position of relative weakness. I wasn't riding a white stallion into the Asian Cup, off the back of consecutive international victories or anything like that. We hadn't won for ages, but that didn't change the responsibility to be bold. As far as I see it, that run of losses was the management equivalent of having metrics that are down. But you don't change course because of 'down' periods that you know to be temporary.

I couldn't change course on the players because we'd have ended up stranded in a dead calm somewhere. I wasn't going to react to the pressure because I knew where we were going and what was required to reach our target. Football deserves leadership that goes beyond metrics. Such is the energy stored in the huge football community that committed, visionary thinking and behaviour will unleash those huge pent-up reserves. I believe that with this type of mentality, the metrics will be washed away in a tsunami of positive responses from the football community. Give them something to chase, something towards which they can build, something that will make their dreams come to life. Empower them and just see how quickly it can happen.

Football has the most important of commodities: people. With people onside and energised, mountains can be moved. Football people know how big their game is and how big its potential is. They want words and pictures and energy, not flaccid corporate speak. Anything less won't inspire them or recruit them to the cause. They won't stick with something leaders don't believe in or are nervous about, they'll see straight through it.

I want the A-League, and football in general, to have a marquee approach to everything, not just the recruitment of a player here or there. I view the current marquee concept in exactly the same way as I do my coaching: there's something more meaningful than wins and losses. That is, a scramble to acquire suitable star players in order to increase ticket sales and TV ratings is the same as a manager fixated on winning and losing. If a club sought to recruit star players who fit hand-in-glove with the story that club wanted to tell about itself, over the course of the journey everything would automatically go to another level.

Unfortunately, in my view, we've adopted the former method; a sort of patchwork approach to finding players here or there with, as I've said, very mixed results at best. The game should believe excellence is achievable. Star players will be attracted by the inexorable growth of the game, not the other way around. The challenge is for clubs to identify players who fit into the storytelling of their own bigger-picture narrative. That is a powerful combination.

As I've found at every step of my football journey, you'll only get where you want to go if you can find some special meaning in it. You've got to find the story you want to tell and then pursue it relentlessly.

The story of a young and untested squad that prove themselves against the best teams on the planet in the crucible of the World Cup finals. The also-rans that transform into a record-setting, possession-based football team that dominates the league. A national team that, under extraordinary pressure, becomes champion of an entire continent for the first time. A domestic game that boldly and ambitiously grows and grows, sweeping up all who adore it along the way. A Greek migrant boy who longs to be close to his father and, in changing Australian football for the better, finds meaning and the place he belongs.

Acknowledgements

It was Nick Fordham and the Fordham family who encouraged me to explore a book like this. I wasn't ready to write an autobiography, but I figured if a family so steeped in the Australian sporting culture was interested in what I had to say about the state of the game, maybe others would like to hear about that as well. Everyone at Penguin then made the seemingly challenging a real possibility.

There are so many people to thank for the journey so far. The ironic thing is that the game has been pivotal to it all. Just about all my friendships have originated from a shared passion or experience on a football field somewhere and, while the bonds have now moved beyond just the game, there is no doubt that is where the roots lie. They are friends for life.

Thanks must also go to the players and coaches who have been with me. I am not one to form close bonds with those I share a workspace with but that does not diminish their impact on me. There is no greater feeling than, once something is accomplished, being able to look around and know that everyone involved has been rewarded for taking a leap of faith. It is another bond for life.

My parents and sister were the protagonists in all of this. My father, who to this day is the only person whose criticism can get under my skin, is the bedrock of my love of the game. It is a simple equation: I loved the game because it got me closer to him, and the rest just evolved from there.

My mum and sister were, I guess, unwitting or unwilling passengers in this. But without their support and encouragement, my father's tough love may have been too much.

To my three boys – James, Max and Alexi – I know their notion of what a dad is is probably different from most others'. Long absences due to the role I hold have meant I have missed a fair bit in their lives so far, but they are the driving force behind everything I do. I look forward to the day when the four of us can sit down and enjoy the game the same way I did with my dad.

The game has made all this happen. Family, friendships and experiences beyond my wildest imagination. However the greatest gift it has given me is introducing me to my wife, Georgia. When the person beside you believes in you more than you can ever imagine believing in yourself, the road ahead doesn't hold any fears. I love you, beautiful girl.

Co-author's Note

When the NSL ran its last race in 2003–04, I was assistant coach to Jean-Paul de Marigny at Marconi, moving out of a life as a PE teacher and, as it happened, into a life that would be taken over by football. Preparing ourselves for training one afternoon, JP announced that he had been invited by Ange Postecoglou to assist him on a short tour of France and Belgium with the national Under 20s team. A couple of days later, my phone rang. On the other end was Ange. Other than very cursory acknowledgements at the end of games between us through the NSL years ('well played', 'good game', that sort of thing), I had never had a conversation with him. It turned out that this one wasn't going to be much more expansive, with Ange quickly getting to the point and asking if I wanted to manage the team for that European tour. I couldn't say yes quickly enough.

That single experience told me a lot about Ange. He'd made assessments of me from a distance, and probably in part via the television work I'd been doing.

On the tour, I was privileged to have a ringside seat, observing how he did things. When in this book he describes his coaching and management techniques, the cold fields of France and Belgium circa 2004 leap back into my mind. He's a more refined beast now, but the patterns were clear. We had a couple of ripper laughs on that tour, but otherwise I was left to do my thing and hope it passed muster.

Ange Postecoglou reckons he's fortunate to have had a life in football. Ditto me. Being in a position to share experiences and opinions with people such as Ange has made for an incredibly enriching life. Ange mightn't subscribe to the luck theory, but I do feel extremely fortunate. Working on this book, with him, telling his story, is but the latest example.

Andy Harper

About the Co-author

Andy Harper played 321 NSL games over fifteen years, scoring 101 goals and winning a championship with Marconi in 1993. A PE teacher by training, he has moved full-time into football, primarily on television – he has worked as a commentator and show host for Fox Sports for a decade. Harper has covered five FIFA World Cup finals, from France in 1998 to Brazil in 2014, and Australia's three Asian Cup tournaments, including the Socceroos' final appearances in 2011 and 2015. He has coached and consulted at various levels, up to the NSL and the FFA.

Harper is also a published author, including co-writing the late Johnny Warren's bestselling biography *Sheilas, Wogs and Poofters*. *Changing the Game* is his fourth book.